THE WREN THE MIND ALLOWS TO SING

A colloquium concerning itself
with Peter O'Leary's trilogy:

Phosphorescence of Thought,
Earth Is Best
The Hidden Eyes of Things

Dan Beachy-Quick
Billie Chernicoff
Norman Finkelstein
Elizabeth T. Gray, Jr.
Whit Griffin
Devin Johnston
Emily Tristan Jones
Devin King
Márton Koppány
Steven Manuel
Thomas Meyer
Patrick Morrissey
Michael O'Leary
Peter O'Leary
Kylan Rice
John Tipton
Steven Toussaint
G. C. Waldrep
Stephen Williams

DOS MADRES
2025

DOS MADRES PRESS INC.
P.O. Box 294, Loveland, Ohio 45140
www.dosmadres.com   editor@dosmadres.com

Dos Madres is dedicated to the belief that the small press is essential to the vitality of contemporary literature as a carrier of the new voice, as well as the older, sometimes forgotten voices of the past. And in an ever more virtual world, to the creation of fine books pleasing to the eye and hand.

Dos Madres is named in honor of Vera Murphy and Libbie Hughes, the "Dos Madres" whose contributions have made this press possible.

Dos Madres Press, Inc. is an Ohio Not For Profit Corporation and a 501 (c) (3) qualified public charity. Contributions are tax deductible.

Executive Editor: Robert J. Murphy

Illustration & Book Design: Elizabeth H. Murphy
www.illusionstudios.net

Cover: "The Great Carolina Wren" (detail) by John Lames Audubon published 1827 is in the public domain.

"Ataxia: Aids Is Fun", 1993, Derek Jarman. Tate.
Used with permission of the Keith Collins Will Trust. Photo: Tate.

Typeset in Adobe Garamond Pro & Bastliga One
ISBN 978-1-962847-22-3
Library of Congress Control Number: 2025936410

First Edition

WE set out to read the three books of Peter O'Leary's trilogy on consciousness: *Phosphorescence of Thought*, *Earth Is Best* and *The Hidden Eyes of Things*. Read we did, thoughtful and mirthful, from the 1st of May through the 9th of June, 2023, 40 days and 40 nights.

Here is our logbook, and our dove.

Billie Chernicoff
12 June 2023

INTRODUCTION

Latter-day Goethe. It fits. The natural world, mushrooms and birds, the classical, Peter's Latin and Greek, his soulful sojourn in Vienna an "Italian Journey." Or so we discover in this colloquy when dialogue resounds rather than resolves. A Time Machine, it feels like, returning to Berkeley in the late fifties with Jack Spicer, Robert Duncan, Robin Blaser, and thus, to that last serrated edge of Modernism. Still shaken to the core by Yeats's late poems, especially compared to Pound's *Personae* and the impending fragmentation of his *Cantos* alongside Eliot's midlife abandonment of poetry. Nearly wrecked upon this reef, we see the lighthouse in time, manned by Charles Olson, and how our poetry can contain a prospect, it can, it will be a projection in and of its glorious self.

Back to Goethe. Peter's three books stand in this fantasia like bins holding large patches of Venetian Epigrams, *Faust* Part II, physical color theory. Time is to be thanked for allowing what Melville did with "matter" to turn *Earth Is Best* into poetry. It was obvious by the time Peter addressed the gathered via Zoom that those of us in this enterprise were looking for contours, dealing with plasticity, not anything carved, cut, or dried.

I remember as a dewy nineteen-year-old visiting Olson at Fort Square with Gerrit Lansing. He'd just received in the mail typescripts from Duncan of what would become "Passages." He waved the pages at us, wowed by the accomplishment, their irreconcilable beauty, a real Walter Pater moment. There the poem lay with its glittering, jeweled interior like a geode. That was a long time ago, yet still today Peter's trilogy begs, not argument, but vista. Talking about his work we come to serious issues like Christianity. We thought that had been settled by now. Struck was I by the title and the homophone "aloud" and "allowed." Finger to the lips, utter not the mystery? Intriguing that our discourse is aesthetic nonetheless objective. Yet never subjective, always solid: *The most beautiful thing I leave is sunlight. Second the shining stars and face of the moon. Then ripe cucumbers, apples, and pears too.* To quote one of the only remaining passages by Praxilla, mid fifth century BCE. Her cucumbers inspired a Greek proverb, "sillier than Adonis." We are still there, as a culture, trivializing the mundane while promoting the representative. Just as exemplary is Peter's refusal to mouth plain, simple, clear-cut English. His rhetoric is just that, it resounds, it resumes. Its word orders (subject / verb / object) seek variation to shake things up, never fusty though. Or frumpy or "antique."

What really impresses herein is the company Peter keeps. The level of conversation, back and forth, the subtle participations, word, paragraph, proposal. Not so much brain storms as brain waves. Smart, never dismissive.

I confess, I've waited for Peter all my adult life, stinging from a reading I gave during the late seventies in Washington DC where the hip poets in the audience were aghast at my quoting Dorothy Wordsworth's diaries. Suffering faint praise for my musicality, in effect damning my content, flowers and folklore. As then, I still believe the stuff of poetry comes from everywhere. Do I mean, anywhere? Any way?

Again, this work we've been pondering never loses its tensegrity, to invoke Buckminster Fuller. Its openness is a fretwork at times. Close weave at others. Caution, I tell myself, looking at the brilliance of critical approach and amplifying notation, the voices joined herein. Is this the charisma of age? No, just aging. To realize the world as a nine-year-old once aspired to, that of Bennet Cerf and Arlene Frances, mid-century Manhattan. Scary, long night, we endured before the dawn of pop art. No, this isn't self-indulgence on my part, Peter's range of voices sideswipes gangster movies and Spenser's *Faerie Queene* to our shared delight.

—Thomas Meyer

THE WREN THE MIND ALLOWS TO SING

We now begin our study of the mind
within. Let us use the words *psychic overtone*,
suffusion, or *fringe*.

Let us
speak in whispers of the one,
of the meticulous hinge
on the Book of Knowledge hidden in rapt

prelude. Apart. Come.

Let us use the word *re-entry*.
Let us sing the differentiating motions
whereby thought's signals
slide in runnels
down the mind's
great glacial expanse

pooling
at the base, lubricating
its massive shelves, its agonized
calves. Let us use
the word *epistrophe*
to mean the turning back of otherwise organized energy
to the supra-organized
diadem of the Godhead—premeditative acts
of prayer. Pre-

cognitive flights of birds.

— Peter O'Leary, *Phosphorescence of Thought* (5-7)

[Billie Chernicoff, Catskill, NY]

Hi all,

Possibly to begin:

In *The Great Code: The Bible and Literature,* Northrop Frye writes:

> The linguistic idiom of the Bible . . . is not metaphorical like poetry, though it is full of metaphor, and is as poetic as it can well be without actually being a work of literature. It does not use the transcendental language of abstraction and analogy, and its use of objective and descriptive language is incidental throughout. It is really a fourth form of expression, for which I adopt the now well-established term *kerygma,* proclamation. (29)

Kerygma, Frye continues, is a mode of rhetoric, but unlike other modes of rhetoric, it does not make an argument, but instead acts as "the vehicle of what is traditionally called revelation" (29).

Peter's work makes a similar claim for itself: "*et clamavit voce magna*" (*Hidden Eyes,* 25). The work is, I believe, not only religious in terms of its frame of reference, which would describe the work of many poets. Rather, it is specifically Christian—however idiosyncratic its Christianity may be—in terms of *what it wants to make happen in the world.* This sets it apart, for better or worse, from almost all its contemporaries.

Related to the work's kerygmatic aspiration is the apparent absence of doubt in it. For many Christians who are intellectuals, to be religious *is* to doubt. Fanny Howe's doubt is nothing less than the matrix of the human world. But Peter's work evinces, so far as I can tell, zero doubt as to the reality of God. The *nature* of God may be an open question, but the fact of God is not.

It might be interesting then to consider how the kerygmatic mode relates to the modes of experimental poetry the work participates in—modes derived from Anglo-American modernism and from *The New American Poetry* and its followers. These modes, particularly in their more latter-day forms, emphasize, precisely, doubt and unknowing (Duncan's "endarkenment"), multiplicity ("all parts of the poem [are] polysemous"), process, digression, deferral, and the vertiginous sense of being "in the open" (I'm thinking here in particular of Michael Palmer's talk from the 2019 Paris Duncan conference, "Coda: The Open"). Poets in this tradition are often interested in the sacred, but rarely committed to religious institutions.

All of this would seem inhospitable to proclamation. It might be interesting then to think more deeply about how these two modes, the kerygmatic mode and the (for lack of an apter term) experimental mode, work together and against one another in Peter's work.

[Stephen Williams, Chicago]

This is fascinating and, I think, a productive way to read Peter's work. I'm wondering, though, Stephen, if the kerygma is itself a radical—an *experimental*—gesture. Peter's unshakable faith is nervy and wildly unpopular and puts him in the open. What do you think?

[John Tipton, Chicago]

Also for starters:

Moneybags

Does the O'Leary Trilogy offend the reader's spiritual and poetic proprieties? Is its superfluity of diction a matter of generosity, or recklessness? Surely it is worship of the one true God. But are the words also being hoarded? And is it the work of a shaman, or just a layman dabbling in spirits? The new soberness of the final installment suggests the former. If spells are cast, is it in one's own reading of the text? In what danger does any of this put us? And what Catholic danger? Are not these poems to be believed? I hereby give to Peter O'Leary his shaman name: Moneybags.

[Emily Tristan Jones, Montreal]

Bare Bones

Two overlapping rhetorics which result in a third (set theory).

Wordsworth: lyric landscape (birds) (1)

Buckmaster Fuller: technology (physics) (2)

Didactic vs Deixis: Blake + Whitman (visionary) (3)

[Thomas Meyer, Cumberland, UK]

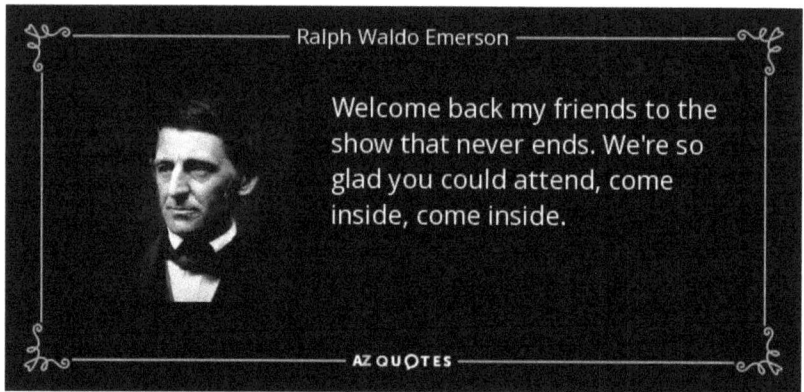

Ralph Waldo Emerson

Welcome back my friends to the show that never ends. We're so glad you could attend, come inside, come inside.

AZ QUOTES

[Devin King, Oxford]

On the lyric landscape and birds: This poem is modeled closely on *Leaves of Grass*, from anaphoric incantations to its varieties of diction to its very length in lines. But like Tom, I also think of Wordsworth: Peter's wren for the "wandering Voice" of the cuckoo, his Des Plaines for Wordsworth's Yarrow, the Romantic mind made manifest through nature. Throughout *Phosphorescence of Thought*, I hear modulations between lyrical balladry of Wordsworth and a Whitmanian mode. The poem opens with the wren's song, in iambic lines that could have been cast in tetrameter: "The wren the mind allows to sing / alights—and flits—on branches bare," with the interior rhyme of "sing" with "anything." Then the lines stretch out, the rhythms complicate, the syntax enters little knots and eddies (Peter's characteristic use of propositions to close a line or phrase: "the woods at dusk flood with," "like sutras meditators seep their thoughts in . . ." The diction thickens, the river froths with pollutants, with "cottony lutrid foam" that would probably invite Whitman to strip down for a dip.

[Devin Johnston, St. Louis]

And like Whitman and Wordsworth, Peter is a poet of sympathy. He perceives differences—in *Phosphorescence*, especially differences between species—and imagines forms of fellowship that both acknowledge and make contact across distances: "What's it like to be a falcon? / As strange as being a man, and / as idiomatic—." From here the poem seeks to discern kestrel-ness in rapturous, cascading analogies, each another angle of/on the bird, each an adjustment or revision of human vision in terms of how the bird sees. Human terms are what we have to see with—each species' terms for the world as private or peculiar as another's—but in attempting to cross idioms, Peter achieves a deeper strangeness of vision. Through his weird binoculars we see both the bird and ourselves startlingly anew: "Imagine / the words of your thoughts dropping from your ears onto / the pavement, piled there."

In other passages, Peter's sympathy manifests in moving tenderness, as when he bears witness to the endangered

Kirtland's warbler: "Little / latter-day survivor. / Little memory remnant of the forest world. / Little once-abundant mystery streamer. / Little prodigious / migrator. Little signaler of the end of days." This is apocalyptic ecology—a vision of both destruction and persistence, rendered with loving sweetness. I remember the time ol' Moneybags and I glimpsed a Kirtland's warbler in downtown Chicago—

[Patrick Morrissey, Chicago]

Somewhat following in Devin's footsteps, I want to begin simply by thinking about the beginning:

The wren
the mind
allows
to sing
alights
—and flits—
on branches bare

Curious that the precondition for the wren's song isn't the wren itself but the mind's allowance. I hear here one aspect of the faith I find mining (& minding) itself through the trilogy as a whole, perhaps a poetic faith more than a Christian one (though thought of *logos* writ large might alter that assumption), in which mind establishes or founds a relational world in which the sound the wren makes becomes song. I feel here a radical interdependence of attention, where imagination furthers the reality it participates in, builds a world that can move from the disyllabic (& lovely, somehow, that there is no monosyllable, as if the poem opens with the implicit understanding that nothing can live alone) to the disyllabic doubled, as if true attention keeps repeating the world in greater measure, increasing the possibilities of utterance and so also of song.

But then, first page of *Phosphorescence* still:

embankments men pile up
to keep
the river
tame.

Another use of mind, one that tames nature instead of wilding it into order of vaster kind (song). & the monosyllable there, "tame," which feels it hardly knows how to give birth to the next utterance. A warning or premonition about the mind's double nature? & so language's, too?

[Dan Beachy-Quick, Fort Collins, CO]

What bullshit!
Even so, you love it, the prog-rock
liner notes of it. Every word.

The Hidden Eyes of Things, page 135

Peter is funny! Like Elric of Melniboné, or prog-rock liner notes, or "silly Celtic lore," or "canst thou draw out leviathan with an hook?" He rocks. His visionary moments suffused with infectious glee. The speaker of the coda of *Phosphorescence of Thought* sounds to me like a man on whom revelation has landed like a punchline: an image of all that is elevated, debased, miraculous, and unnecessary about human intelligence embodied in a "troglodytic wren" in a "shabby little Forest Preserve." Wildly mismatched scales of being that nevertheless cohere like a skinny man in an enormous suit. The poet is so inspired he addresses the object of his vision in the same teasing tone of voice he might use to address his cat:

> Little hole-dwelling soul.
> Wren-thin omen offered the world.
> Your soul's little mineral mood.
> Little soul of the body of the earth.
> Little emerald murmur; little mineral myrrh.
> The earth's self-borne law.
> Its gravitous autochthonomy. Its beardedness.
> Its leathery elementation. Its keen aquiline piggy-backing.
> Its excessive tiny intelligence.

[Brendan White, Chicago, Illinois]

Phosphorescence and, differently, *Earth Is Best*, are both field books: they take note of the world while immersed in it. Hence, perhaps, Peter's use of the fragment and the list, a jotting-down while on the move. And yet, especially in light of the second and third installments of the Trilogy, the fragment has a summoning or presencing power. It doesn't function like a fragment as I normally think of it— incomplete, jittery, nervous, open-ended; instead, in Peter's work, it indicates solidity, unit, unity, rondure, closure, presence beyond grammar, beyond language, even, which falls quiet almost as soon as uttered, so as to simply (austerely) observe. Observation is observance, reverence in the face of something permanent, durable. Peter's nouns shorn of syntax feel infinitive. They do what Eliot describes, "investing form with lucid stillness / Turning shadow into transient beauty / With slow rotation suggesting permanence."

[Kylan Rice, Saxapahaw, NC]

Peter's verse is a poetry of electricities. Charges fire across synapses—his and the reader's—and radiate from the page. In this trilogy exploring consciousness, he thickens the act of thinking and manifests it to the reader. He deploys an array of formal strategies but there are two syntactic moves, I believe, that are particularly effective in this regard.

First, the complex grammar Devin Johnston notes above. Specifically, Peter unfurls long and involved relative clauses—often with nested subordinate clauses of their own—without using a relative pronoun to signal the shift out of the main clause. It's become one of his signature moves:

An accidental eternity the lake's waves swell with mist enlumes
    in aerosol.
                    "Twenty-Third Amanita Ode," *Earth Is Best*

When L laces every porous tubule gametes strobe from like
    sugar shook from a caster.
                    "Ochre Vault," *Earth Is Best*

The bewildered reader has to hunt for the object of the preposition or parse out the subject and verb of the main clause. Nothing makes sense until we reach the end and the entire looping construction comes together with a jolt of sense. Along the way, the dazzling and curious diction adds to the disorientation, making the resolution at the end all the more satisfying. Each one of these produces a small revelation in the reader's mind.

Second (also noted by Kylan Rice), Peter will deploy a series of short, often verbless statements or fragments ended with a period. It's a strategy most evident in *The Sampo* but he's told me that he first developed it in "The Dogs" in *Earth Is Best* (Peter's version of the Actaeon story in Book Three of the *Metamorphoses*, a poem written before *The Sampo*, though published later). The effect is cubist—a layering of glimpses that form a composite:

His pleas to his dogs: a stag's braying. They charge
eagerly after. Actaeon submerged in animal. All verb. All
    summons.
Resonant aether. It's the Black Slayer first.

At first, the staccato of short bursts is unsettling. But it quickly becomes evident that the period isn't a stop, it's a connector for a catenary of observations and events. The frequent periods have the counterintuitive effect of accelerating the lines—the poem becomes telegraphic and urgent. The reader has to keep up. And we are amazed, which, I believe, is an altered state of consciousness.

[John Tipton]

Kerygma and experimental poetry

What if we bring up Blake as a kerygmatic, experimental poet as comparison? (Frank Samperi is another—more recently contemporary, esp. with his own *Trilogy* not out but a few years back—poet we might think of.)

I'm thinking of this paragraph in Gordon Teskey's *The Poetry of John Milton* (a book I know Peter admires, has used while teaching both Milton and Blake), page 292:

> From what has been said so far
> it should be clear that Blake is the only
> Romantic poet to engage Milton on the terms
> Milton himself thought most important:
> those of Christianity. Coleridge, Wordsworth,
> Shelley, Keats, and Byron all admire Milton's
> political morals and especially his principled
> firmness during the English Revolution and
> after, during the Restoration, when the poet
> was "in darkness and with dangers compassed
> round" (*PL*, 7.27). But Milton's Christianity
> is an embarrassment to them. What was most
> important to Milton, when he justified the
> ways of God to men, was the coming kingdom
> of God on earth, which would occur not by
> the vindication of principles and rights but by
> the Second Coming of Christ. It is Christ, and
> not a better version of the French Revolution,
> that will bring in final justice . . .

This seems to set up a reading of the kerygmatical poet as an experimental one (thinking here of Tipton's reply above

13

to the opening paragraphs/questions). Coleridge was an "endarkened" poet, but also highly drawn to abstraction and rumination. Wordsworth was pious, neo-Platonic, Christian, worshipful of nature. Keats and Shelley were pagans (Shelley a pagan, a neo-Platonist; translation of *the Banquet*, Thomas Taylor there) and the second of those two was (somehow) both radically skeptical and radically vatic. Byron is something else; though he's one of the Romantics, he's also indebted heavily to Horace, and probably Horace-by-way-of-Pope's-*Imitations*. So you're a far way off from kerygma there.

Looking at this with some historical comparison, I wonder if it makes Peter's position as kerygmatic and also experimental poet clearer?

I don't have a fully formed sense of an argument here; I'm just writing what came into my head on thinking about this over the last few days.

One extra-literary comparison also flew to mind: Arvo Pärt.

[Steven Manuel, Providence, RI]

━━━━━━━━━━━━━━━━━━━━━━━━━━━━━━━━━━━━━

a) syntax ("double-jointed syntax")
b) prosody (the word, early on; here in these books (starting with *Depth Theology*), the line or sentence); who, aside from Whitman, is the main force? the (pivotal or exemplary) prosody of *The Sampo*: imagist, narrative epic*
c) structural form (over long poems taking up books: Taggart is maybe most important here, at least with *Phos*.)
d) relation of David Jones—Stephen Williams already

brought this up with the "order of signs"—to Peter/ both their work aside one another?

* People can check out the interview from a few years ago I conducted with Peter at "Stray Horn," my blog. In retrospect, I asked jackass questions.

[Steven Manuel]

It's probably important to note that Mercury went retrograde on April 21 and will move out of retrograde on May 14. That fact will undoubtedly exert an influence over this conversation.

[John Tipton]

I am rereading each book in chronological order, having read all of them several times, first in manuscript and then in print. So while the rest of you are already moving onwards/upwards towards *Earth Is Best* and *The Hidden Eyes of Things,* I am still meditating on *Phosphorescence of Thought,* which is the furthest back in my own reading.

I'm interested in the cataloging aspect of Peter's work, and the way cataloging relates to praise. Because *Phosphorescence* is explicitly a poem of praise, as it is also a poem of making: "Make holy / all you works of God with praise and exultation" (27), which heads the 5.5-pp. praise-litany cast in the second person. (We are, sometimes, cast in the second person.)

One can imagine a space (a poem) of pure praise. And yet praise here is the hinge or buckle, and not the end, not the fulfillment. "*If you abolish the symbols, then you tear down the walls of your own house,*" the poem asserts—and then the question, "*What is this fearsome mystery fulfilling itself in me?*"

What interests me perhaps is the poem's recognition that praise takes place in *time*, that "fearsome mystery"—whatever that is—not only fulfills itself (in me!), but is "fulfilling" itself in me, so that an ongoing action (enactment) is defining the time it inhabits, autochthonously (or autochthonomously, as Peter coins here). There is space inside of, or just outside of, just beyond, praise in which the -ing happens, whether it be "fulfilling" or some other action, that propels forward, in a time-space defined by this propellant motion. Things happen there. Some of those things are symbols, the fields of resonant phenomena we label "symbols."

So the symbol is a happening, an event both defined in and by time and pushing outward from time, our sense of time, into new time, time as yet unexperienced, unexpended.

There are also "houses," those charities, but I am not as certain about them, not yet (pax Bachelard).

And there is the Franciscan aspect of this work—of the essential charity of this work (cf. "Sister Moon" on page 45)—an angle of Peter's work that I have never really heard anyone discuss. Perhaps it's most evident here, in this book? The sense that there is "some law," something called law (48), but that we are not creatures of it, we are *in its presence,* co-presences.

[G.C. Waldrep, Lewisburg, Pa.]

This in response primarily to John's comments above—those following my initial contribution—

It's hard for me to imagine an avant-garde or modernist Christianity. That's what makes Peter's work both compelling and vexing for me.

There's experimental with respect to other poetry, and then there's radical with respect to reality. Peter's poetry is radical with respect to reality. The gospel message is radical with respect to reality, though Christianity itself, as a historical and cultural reality, is another matter. But I don't really buy the argument that Christianity's wild unpopularity makes Peter's embrace of it especially remarkable *in itself.* This is essentially an argument for the Christian poet as modernist iconoclast. Over the years I've heard Peter advance two arguments about why Christian poetry is unpopular: people, especially those who are products of universities, lack imagination, and they lack conviction in the face of the secular zeitgeist. In this way they stand for "bourgeois taste" in the old modernist narrative. [The two arguments are Peter's, paraphrased by me; the connection to modernist iconoclasm is mine, though I think implicit in his thinking.] Okay, there's truth in that; but the real reason people don't embrace Christianity is because they made a sound, adult, totally legitimate decision that it is not for them. The secular zeitgeist—modernity—is just the sum total of those people making that decision.

Be that as it may, and to paint in very broad but, I think, accurate strokes: The New American Poetry is about eliminating hierarchy (even if it failed to do this as a social formation): the open field, etc; Christianity is about submitting to it and honoring it. (Hierarchy is originally a theological term, is it not?) It's as logocentric as it gets. Can one both eliminate hierarchy and submit to it at the same time? And do so in poetry? Logically, no; but poetry allows us to proceed other than logically, and so, inasmuch as Peter pulls it off, I am curious as to the dialectical or spiritual maneuvers involved.

Or think about the phantastikon. For Duncan, Spicer, et al., whatever comes up is what comes up: Vermont and Vietnam are equally valid. Whereas in a Christian situation one of the signs is, as George Orwell would say, more equal than all the others. How can these impulses be reconciled in a way that fulfills both and compromises neither? This is not a rhetorical question.

*

It's as if he's taken projective verse and aimed it up instead of out.

*

Reading the work, it has occurred to me how the great English-language poets of Christianity are all the most physical: I struck the board and cried No more, Batter my heart, break blow burn, Milton's rolling thunder pentameter, Hopkins's instress. Fanny Howe's ecstatic lash. They're always slamming up against matter. Why is this? I don't know, but perhaps it's that the kerygmatic force of the address requires an equal (and opposite?) counterforce to work against, or else . . .

*

Even though the three books under consideration take a conspicuous turn away from theological language and reference of *Luminous Epinoia*—and this turn might be an interesting topic for discussion—Christianity is essential to the work. One cannot "read through" it as if it were a student's grammar error, much as one might like to if, like Coleridge, Wordsworth, etc., one finds it embarrassing—*cf* the Teskey quote above. Peter once said that the "Christos mythos" is for him what the Orpheus myth is for Ronald Johnson. Or, if you don't believe me, hear it from the man himself. Go to 1:16:16. [See "Thick and Dazzling Darkness."] Note that this talk takes place under the auspices of the *Lumen Christi Institute*.

And kerygma by definition demands that you say yes or no. No one ever shrugs in the New Testament; no one ever says "you do you," no one ever says "on the other hand." This, then, is the risky thing about what Peter's doing, it seems to me: *forcing the issue* where most poets (including me, and I'm not saying it's a bad thing) try to defer, and valorize that deferral. The real risk is not that people will dismiss the work *itself* out of casual bigotry, but that they will reject *what the work proposes* or proclaims out of careful and considered thought. But when they do so, they're not rejecting the work; on the contrary, they (we) are taking it up on its own terms.

[Stephen Williams]

The kerygma is not just some poetic device. It is central to Catholic evangelization. It needs to be said that Peter is an evangelist. When Christian evangelism is off-putting to us, this is not just because of its style, but because of the claims it makes.

Of course, Catholicism has loads of room for doubt. But we all already do that in buckets. (And it is the cool poetic device too.)

I'm asking very earnestly: is Peter dabbling in spirits?????????????????????

[Emily Tristan Jones]

Stephen (and John)—thanks for this. I am thinking about kerygma and doubt as two axes of whatever it is we are talking about when we invoke "Christian poetry." I personally would make Incarnation the third axis—that makes the model three-dimensional—although I am not sure whether Peter's work posits this particular third axis. (Your comments re. the physicality/sensuality of the greatest Christian poetry do I think underscore this point.)

I simply don't see the doubt axis as operative in Peter's poetry, as an aspect of the work; it may be a latent axis, or entirely absent. So my question is, if we recognize the proclamatory or kerygmatic axis, what other axes are there?

I might hazard that *decay* is one—whether in the lutrid/ lutrescent coinage of *Phosphorescence* or in the mycological focus of *Earth Is Best*. (I can't work this out yet in terms of *Hidden Eyes*.) There is also of course the tension between what is "hidden" and what is observable, shared, praise-able: but I don't think this is an "axis," I think it's an underlying tension (that in some way or ways unifies his conceptions of the spiritual and the material).

I'm not sure kerygma "by definition demands that you say yes or no." Logically it does, but as you point out, poems can proceed by paths other than those logic remands. Perhaps it's possible to conceive of *Phosphorescence* in particular as an exercise in a kerygma that self-posits a range of possible responses, even as it inserts itself, as every poem must, into the order of signs.

[G.C. Waldrep]

I live in Canada where such unabashedly Christian poetry has no place unless in a Christian bookshop, published by a Catholic press (American), and maybe it has the photo of a burning candle on glossy cover paper. In any case, this trilogy wouldn't have a fighting chance here, whether among the savvy secular poets, or churchgoers. Beautifully designed books out of Brooklyn, discussed by the twenty-five of us here isn't what counts as wildly unpopular (John Tipton). Does it need a major press? Would a major press not publish this stuff because it is Christian or because it has zero doubt (Stephen Williams)? There is Christian poetry that is palatable, excusable, understandable, relatable. And then there is unabashed proclamation, which can be embarrassing, and off-putting to readers (or associated with rightwing evangelism). But Peter's poetry is kind, exciting, and sensational (especially next to so much stuffy and self-satisfied poetry these days). So, how much can we be moved by this poetry before we begin to believe it? And what do we do with it when we don't? Those are the things that I want to know. If we don't believe these poems, then I guess they are only good for excitement and sensation. To which I say, who cares.

[Emily Tristan Jones]

"So, how much can we be moved by this poetry before we begin to believe it? And what do we do with it when we don't? Those are the things that I want to know." I like the way, Emily, that this broaches the either/or of kerygma that Stephen asserts. And in fact this is my precise reaction, not to Peter's work, but to Whitman's—a spectrum of reactions that mediate between aesthetic response ("being moved," but not only that) and belief (or in my case, disbelief, perhaps a radical disbelief, in Whitman's vision).

But there's another question embedded in what you say here, which is perhaps my own central question and dread as a poet: what place is there in culture for a poetics that takes belief seriously but does not align with traditional devotional modes (within whatever "tradition"). I think you're right that it's the explicit expression of doubt that makes *some* "Christian poetry" palatable to a wider audience—but I have to admit I'm weary of a Christian poetics that circles doubt exclusively, explicitly, and relentlessly.

All of which is perhaps a detour from the main movement of this conversation, but—perhaps not. What praise does, as a rhetorical vector, is perhaps to bypass "belief," as such. It may proceed from belief, but the terms on which it demands to be read or evaluated are not those of belief. My own best guess about Peter's work's lack of reception is that it foregoes narrative (pax *Sampo*). And, all that crazy diction! (I well remember rifling through multiple dictionaries for "lutrescent," "lutrid," etc. when Peter first shared the completed manuscript of *Phosphorescence* with me in 2011 or 2012. That was before he added his note.)

[G.C. Waldrep]

But as I said, I don't think it does lack reception. (Sure, these poems are so good that they should be more popular than they are, but that's just what happens in the arts.) Maybe his poetry is less popular than it should be because of the crazy diction, the missing narrative, and because of the Christianity. But that's also all the stuff that makes it so good. The Christianity is surely a part of that.

[Emily Tristan Jones]

Not using that phrase, in scare quotes, to question whether Peter's work should be considered Christian poetry—using it to highlight that there is a "Christian poetry" community, even industry, out there, to which neither Peter nor (to my knowledge) anyone else here is a party. . . . But yes, of course that's what makes it good! Is why we are here, having this wonderful conversation.

Maybe a more interesting question is *how* Peter's work is Christian poetry (with or without the scare quotes). But I also think it responds to and embraces ecologies of discourse that lie outside of that, whatever that is, and I'm interested in those aspects of the work. Not to mention the birds and mushrooms and stars, which substitute for narrative, because . . . they are their own narrative?

[G.C. Waldrep]

But it is Christian poetry. I'm not sure we can so comfortably separate ourselves from that. And look at that cover! I guess we're all part of the Christian poetry "community" now.

[Emily Tristan Jones]

Offering some resonances from other reading I'm doing now which Peter's work wholly in mind, & tied to the mention of Johnson's Orpheus by Stephen, & very curious in general about Orphic tendencies here, that parallel or echo or ride astride or dig underneath the Christological, all from Elizabeth Sewell's (mind-opening & mind-confirming to me) *The Orphic Voice*:

". . . will explore . . . possible relations in the world of nature as perceived by the mind, 'that commerce between the mind of man and the nature of things,' as Bacon said, which needs to be 'restored to its perfect and original condition.'"

*

". . . a mythological vision of the relationship between man's mind and the natural universe."

*

"To see the whole of nature as generative process is part of postlogic, and allows the thinking organism to figure in itself the processes it is reflecting upon."

*

". . . postlogic, which is an operation of mind and language directed toward nature, he is profoundly concerned with the point at which nature and language meet."

*

". . . a life which is also capable of translation into music."

*

The question of language and grammar, the nature of the catalog, opened generously by Kylan and John, feel pressing here. But there is also the music, the muse, the musing—maybe the *amuse*ment, per Brendan—that feels here coming to bear.

[Dan Beachy-Quick]

The Heresiarch's Enchiridion

The foraging way is the visionary way

And the esculent honeycomb of light.
The living symbol. A being of pure light.
You are a raptorial spirit bird. The
angel who sits upon the Tree of Life.

The crystal flickering vision. The vault
and the myth. The roots of the birch
tap into the lake of the Waters of Life.
The new light rising in the radial east.
What dawning finds the vision alive?

Moon plant. Mandrake. Lunetica.
Tree of the Sea. Like the enormous
gills of a salamander. Consider the
salamandrine woman. The wren who
vexed Thoth. Wayfaring wren in
the newly pruned lilac. The waxy
sound of the ruffian wind. Salamandrine choir.

Migrating dragons in sun-wheeling
pageants. A scintillating nimbus.
The wingstrokes of a thousand migrating
songbirds. Your soul's essence is motion.

Ecstasy in the archangelic sigh. And
the ringing of an all-consuming mesocosmic
chord. You have heard the Sun singing
wildly. You've become aware of a
shape in occultation. The curious
foreshapings of the spirit's life.

Out of the cloud of forgetting and
unknowing. Bright choir of
illuminating sunlight. Icons
carved from a ceaseless noise of
thinking. Unlocking all the lore-
craft and knowledge of magic. The
salt of wisdom at the physical
center of the Earth.

This is the song of the hidden
stone possessing a thousand forms.
The crafts and resources contrived

by rebellion. I have eaten all
the books of all the learning. I
will revive the gods with herbs.

The sorcerer of the outer reaches.
What new arts do you bear up from
the inaccessible treasure chamber?
Liturgy of crystal. Words of
fungal networks. The expanding
scribal matrix. Those stellar
networks hatching galaxies.

Vernal silver the house is steeped
in. Smoke of silver coloring another
world. Lemoning moon. Rolling
easily. Deep source of all your
dreams. You enter this new psychic
institution. The subtle body
comes to life. Nights like these,
ours, forever. Who is the magus
of the Moon?

A quantum garment whose vital
raiment clothes you in thinking.
Long-haired ascetics swathed in
wind. Seers draw closed the
silver drape. You wilderness of
silver. Looking in, what did
you learn? What are you burning?
You wore the white gold and you
burned the sage. To burn a
perfume composed of incense and opium.

Bearing the dream to the rhapsodic
line. Human beings are new every day.
The water has a thousand names.
For the books it wants aren't yet written.

Milking rain from the living cloud.
The god of cloud rolls into the
blue. Blue crystal of daylight.
Days of the glorious streaming
sun. Light does not get old.

Tincture from which all the
dead are revived. The eophanic
visionary reality of the dawn world.
Orange summoner. Strange radiator.
You were praying for the distant forms.
The total encounter. Angels weaving
from feeling. Divinity in you.

Life that springs from a secret
seedless source. By this you
have seen the secrets of the Earth
hidden in plain sight. Cryptic
keys turn the bolts unlocking the
sanctuaries where love and destiny
are stored.

A zone of electrically conducting
fluid undergoing convective motion.
Pathways for all the birds. Through
the rocky passes where time is
strangely magnetized. Birds of omen.

An oracle no burning cleans. Vision
of a heavenly form you only find
as feeling.

Astral light of the midnight sun.
Astral light of the noonday darkness.
A ghostly intelligence of allegory.
The eclipse of the Sun-fed lion.
The love you feel is the light of
the sun. What are the dominant
forms of mystery unfolding for
you to understand?

Courser in the boreal forest
belt. In the pine-rioting
northern forests. Let him crown
your head with sprigs of pine.
Radiant as an elf and as strange.

Wandering myself onward along
the water's ridge. White
poplars clinging to the edge
of the pool of memory. And
the pine woods thickening just
beyond. The woods absorbing
echoes. The scent of myrrh
exuded from a tree intoxicates.
Honey flowed from the oaks.

The uncanny allure. The stars'
resplendent mysticism. All
the living stars. Taffy-scented
star magnolia. The gingko at

dusk. Your perfect absorption
into a small glowing rectangle.
Splashed with bliss. Gathering
euphoria. Like a sylph through
the night. Ancient fish and
creatures of the sea lumber and
move. A comet appears in the sky.

[Whit Griffin, Denver, CO]

Whit, I'd love to hear more about "the foraging way" vs. "the wandering way." I hate to go back to something as inflexibly instrumental as "axes," from my former post, but it seems to me this is a potentially fruitful distinction—for apprehending Peter's work and also more generally.

[G.C. Waldrep]

—Hamish Fulton

Voltaire tells a wild and unauthorized story of a farce seen by Milton in Italy, which opened thus: "Let the Rainbow be the Fiddlestick of the Fiddle of Heaven."

…

Milton has the reputation of having been in his youth eminently beautiful, so as to have been called the Lady of his college. His hair, which was of a light brown, parted at the foretop, and hung down upon his shoulders, according to the picture which he has given of Adam. He was, however, not of the heroick stature, but rather below the middle size, according to Mr. Richardson, who mentions him as having narrowly escaped from being "short and thick." He was vigorous and active, and delighted in the exercise of the sword, in which he is related to have been eminently skilful. His weapon was, I believe, not the rapier, but the backsword, of which he recommends the use in his book on Education.

His eyes are said never to have been bright; but, if he was a dexterous fencer, they must have been once quick.

…

The author's design is not, what Theobald has remarked, merely to shew how objects derived their colours from the mind, by representing the operation of the same things upon the gay and the melancholy temper, or upon the same man as he is differently disposed; but rather how, among the successive variety of appearances, every disposition of mind takes hold on those by which it may be gratified.

The *chearful* man hears the lark in the morning; the *pensive* man hears the nightingale in the evening. The *chearful* man sees the cock strut, and hears the horn and hounds echo in

the wood; then walks "not unseen" to observe the glory of
the rising sun or listen to the singing milk-maid, and view
the labours of the plowman and the mower; then casts his
eyes about him over scenes of smiling plenty, and looks up to
the distant tower, the residence of some fair inhabitant: thus
he pursues rural gaiety through a day of labour or of play,
and delights himself at night with the fanciful narratives of
superstitious ignorance.

The *pensive* man at one time walks "unseen" to muse at
midnight, and at another hears the sullen curfew. If the weather
drives him home he sits in a room lighted only by "glowing
embers"; or by a lonely lamp outwatches the North Star to
discover the habitation of separate souls, and varies the shades
of meditation by contemplating the magnificent or pathetick
scenes of tragick and epick poetry. When the morning comes,
a morning gloomy with rain and wind, he walks into the
dark trackless woods, falls asleep by some murmuring water,
and with melancholy enthusiasm expects some dream of
prognostication or some musick played by aerial performers.

—Johnson, *Milton*

[Devin King, Oxford]

(I also have a version of a talk Peter gave about lists that
my wife and I published in a catalogue. I believe Peter read
it before a chapbook was released with all the birds from
Phosphorescence? John or Michael—do you remember?
Anyways, if that's of interest I can email it to the group—it's
quite long to include in here, I think.)

Re. Emily and G.C.'s exchange above—

Peter's uncompromising conviction as to the reality of God
I have always found fascinating, maddening, compelling,
charming, even frightening. It's as self-evident to him that
divinity is incarnate in everything around him as it is to me
that it's not. Both things can't be true! I have sometimes
thought that he must have a Vita Nuova-like origin story
somewhere in his past, but perhaps that would be too easy,
because it would make the religious energy the consequence
of some event, rather than what it seems more properly to be,
which is unaccountable.

Peter's poetry appeals to me for many reasons not directly
related to religion, among them: its atom-splitting
("compression & radiation") approach to language; its
Pollock-like combination of density and velocity; its many
uses of syntax, some of which John and others have pointed
to; the way in which the poems are generally so expansive
and yet any two or three lines could be a magnificent poem
by themselves; the vertiginous ways lines collapse and expand
from very long to very short; the way verbal ornament enacts
natural fluidity and spiritual superfluity; the way the Greek
and Latin of science answer the Greek and Latin of the
Church; the work's recognition that nature is convulsive and
not essentially consoling, idyllic, or salvific; the metaphorical
imagination—the wit; the resourcefulness—with which it
reinvents the Neoplatonic microcosm / macrocosm structure
as mushroom: mind: star.

[Stephen Williams]

re. "he must have a Vita Nuova-like origin story." It's Blake, no? Blake and Plato?

[G.C. Waldrep]

(Real quick: I understand that Peter's poetry is not popular as it should be, but it is poetry after all. Isn't that just how things go? My perspective is obscured here in paltry Canada. Because let me tell you, he wouldn't even be teaching. So, maybe that's why the Catholicism is the wildest part of the work for me. And then in relation to the spells. The magic. I'm pretty sure that Catholics aren't supposed to be doing that! So when we say (G.C.) that the *praise* and the *how* of the Christianity here is what is interesting (plus the birds, mushrooms, and whatnot), it gets me thinking about the magic.

[Emily Tristan Jones]

Some remarks on form:

As noted frequently above, Whitman's influence is evident throughout these three books (and the rest of Peter's work). Lists of declarations, proclamations, and celebrations abound. But the anaphoric observations and praises also bear the marks of Christopher Smart's *Jubilate Agno*:

For I will consider my Cat Jeoffry.
For he is the servant of the Living God duly and daily serving him.

For at the first glance of the glory of God in the East he
worships in his way.
For this is done by wreathing his body seven times round with
elegant quickness.
For then he leaps up to catch the musk, which is the blessing
of God upon his prayer.

Compare *Phosphorescence* (27):

Make holy
all you works of God with praise and exaltation
you angels of God and you heavens, you magnifiers of all the
single quantum's original energy
you hydrogen and helium, you universe of frenzied particles
billowing out
you primordial billion years depthless night shuddered toward
transfiguration through

There are games and generative methods. In a note to Billie,
Liz, and me, Pete tipped us off to a couple compositional
techniques. "Hidden Stone" in *Earth Is Best* opens with an
acrostic, the first seven stanzas spell out *VISITA INTERIORA
TERRAE RECTIFICANDO INVENIES OCCULTUM
LAPIDEM*, "look into the interior of the earth with care(?)
you will find the hidden stone." An alchemical motto and, as
Google tells me, the title of a metal album. It figures, coming
from Pete. He also said there was a method hiding on pages
24–25 of *Phosphorescence*. The lines of the third stanza on
25 open with the words *hankering, gross, mystical, nude*, a
quote from *Leaves of Grass*: "who goes there? hankering, gross,
mystical, and nude; / How is it I extract my strength from the
beef I eat?" Lines I've heard Pete quote many times.

I take so much pleasure in these books because there was joy in their making, joy in their forms.

[John Tipton]

Stray thoughts:

Yes to what John Tipton says about how "amazed . . . is an altered state of mind"—the origin of a cascade (overbrimming, explosion, efflorescence) of altered states: wonder, ardor, love, praise, knowing, surrender, union. As G.C. notes, "things happen" in time "ongoingly"—but they also happen all at once, Rilke's *being in excess, the phosphorescence of thought.* Amazement aroused by *seeing,* as the poetry of Peter's trilogy *sees*—lavishly, meticulously, reverently, ecstatically. We *shall see and we shall love. We shall love and we shall praise.* (St. Augustine, via *Phosphorescence,* 15)

I love Mary as the burning bush in *Phosphorescence,* and I learned a new word, *orant,* how did I not know that word?

True, Stephen, about "the way the Greek and Latin of science mirror the Greek and Latin of the Church." I've been trying to figure out how this poetry's vocabulary makes me feel like I'm not only fluent but ecstatic in Latin. Just as certain Sanskrit syllables are sacred in themselves, Peter's (orthodox and invented) Latin is magical, and makes priests and scientists of us readers. It's the language of the Law too, though it does not make lawyers of us! But maybe decent citizens. The Law, as "some / presentiment of an all energizing / memory."

The chants, the catalogs, are wonders. The "You" passage leaves me breathless . . . likewise "the word" passage, a marvel.

A little bird told me that each line of Whit's poem is foraged from the Trilogy. How gorgeously strange and new he makes them, a practice of the Trilogy itself. *The foraging way is the visionary way . . .*

What do you make of the appearance of the alluring and terrifying, "daemonic" Bromios/Dionysus in *Phosphorescence*? Or the two-line coda at the end of that passage, so suddenly intimate and compassionate, that changes everything.

> You find this mixture of thousands, beloved, this
> riot of flowers let loose, overwhelming.

Stephen said "experimental, for lack of an apter word" and at first I wished we would come up with a better word, because this ardent poetry doesn't seem in the least experimental, but I looked up its origins, and it is apt:

experiment (n.)
mid-14c., "action of observing or testing; an observation, test, or trial;" also "piece of evidence or empirical proof; feat of magic or sorcery," from Old French *esperment* "practical knowledge, cunning; enchantment, magic spell; trial, proof, example; lesson, sign, indication," from Latin *experimentum* "a trial, test, proof, experiment," noun of action from *experiri* "to try, test," from *ex* "out of" (see ex-) + *peritus* "experienced, tested," from PIE *per-yo-*, suffixed form of root *per- (3) "to try, risk."

There's that magic, Emily, intrinsic.

[Billie Chernicoff]

I'd like to pick up on the these persistent questions about "doubt," especially Stephen's most recent comments: Might we be better served if we shift our attention from the dichotomy we are most familiar with today—that between religious/theistic fideism and secular/agnostic skepticism—to a dichotomy within the Christian tradition itself? I am thinking of what Martin Luther peevishly described as the incompatibility between "theologies of glory" and "theologies of the cross." Is it possible that the latter dichotomy better explains the peculiarity of Peter's poetics when compared, not only to general trends in contemporary poetry, but also to other "Christian poetries"? That Peter is not best described as a "Christian poet" but, as Stephen perhaps implied, a "Catholic poet." But, more peculiar still, a Catholic committed to an ultra-high theology of glory, who sees the world, because created and "gifted" and not merely extant and "given," as irradiated with grace "all the way down." Nicholas of Cusa was accused of being a pantheist, though he did not believe himself to be. And he shared something of Peter's syncretism, a common trait among theologians of glory (Peter's recent interlocutor David Bentley Hart comes to mind). Is the scandal of Peter's lack of doubt, in fact, far more scandalous than we thought? We might rather ask, as Luther might have asked, is there room in this poetry for *sin*, for the evident *tragedy* of human life and history that would require the prodigious and interruptive event of the Incarnation of a God that is not continuous with but radically other than creation? I think Peter might be working through this problem in passages like the following. Note the relatively sober formal register when compared with the predominant ecstatic flights.

The world assumes an outward air
it strobes with light it cannot bear
while inside nurtured brightness dims
the visions conjured in its hymns.

What sickness measures forms in thought
a light into whose background fraught
intentions bring unchecked decay:
the source—
                    an earthen corpse—

                                        on which we pray.
                                    (*Phosphorescence,* 50)

Though I doubt this would satisfy a Lutheran. Is sin just finitude?

[Steven Toussaint, Cambridge, UK]

Thinking about how this section from *Phosphorescence of Thought* (chosen by scrolling and pointing, a sort of sortes Sanctorum, the text as diagnosis and medicine) embodies much of what has been discussed, both the poetry's formalities and our various propositions, and is a real transmission, initiatory. I am not the same after reading this passage (and not only this one).

Myth is the narrative metaphor sounds out of melodies
ideas finely tune in consciousness. Icons
carved from a ceaseless noise of thinking. The golden hissing
    notes inside them.

Why does it perceive these sensations? For it has daggered the
   crown of the sun.
Why does it stick to the light? For the soul is an extrusion of
   resins.
Why does it stink of this rottenness? For *the language of God
   has no grammar; it consists only of names.*
Why does it father what is merciful? For its athanatopsis is an
   autarchy.
Why does it mimic knaving wrens? For it changes darkness
   into light in matutinal song.
Why does its pressure flash awareness? For its textures are
   those of ice or cloth.
Why does it make this dazzling sign? For the books it wants
   aren't yet written.
Why does it work itself in friendship? For the Eleontic
   Primordium is the arena of life.
Why is it always current and ancient both? For I live in it.
Why is it mistaking despair for depression? For the seasons,
   one after another, draw out like a music the feeling.
Why is it so conformed to this world? For to be transformed
   by the renewal of your mind

is to be changed in your shape.
Exteriority. Interiority. Ascent.
Why is it a dream-power every night showing thee thine own?
   For a man is the conductor of the whole river of electricity.
                                    (*Phosphorescence*, 19-20)

What the heck is Eleontic Primordium, anyway?

[Billie Chernicoff]

I've gone back to *kerugma*, a word I didn't know, hadn't come across in all my years of translating ancient Greek, just to see what is buried in the Liddell & Scott. Beneath "proclamation" and "announcement (of victory)" is "summons" & summons toward a "reward." The verb *kerussein* likewise holds "to summon, to call" among its meanings. I think I feel this deeply in my return to *Phosphorescence*, a return after many years now, with *Hidden Eyes* so recent in my affections. I can feel in Peter's electric anaphora, in the rapid-fire insistence that each thing in the catalog is wholly its own unique shining forth and yet completely in relation to every other singular spark of existence itself, in the "spooky" entanglements, in the "galactic internal dynamics," this other aspect of *kerugma*. It's one that doesn't exactly feel to me a yes-no proposition to the one who hears it, not if a *summons* or a *summoning* is its deep nature. There I hear the Orphic strand that seems to run occultly underneath the Christian. The melody-myth that moves stones and trees—& so perhaps moves the stones & trees that also are ourselves. I think I only mean to say that I feel in Peter's work such a summoning that isn't a choice, but a helpless, almost fated form of *heedfulness*. The song that calls us back to ourselves as an aspect of the larger cosmos, the same call calling out and into all.

I also hear, strange maybe as it is to say, something sacrificial in Peter's work, that it offers itself as a kind of offering, calls itself into the same heedfulness it calls us—a demonstration, not a decree. I'm thinking in part of the fevered take-down of Zeus in *Phosphorescence* on page 17, the "lavish flesh and

41

savory inners of an ox," that appease a god in order to make a plea for like kindness, though "sorrow and mischief" are the god's plans. The poem feels an offering of a different kind: a summons that summons in itself all it calls to in us. So it doesn't proclaim truth, at least not exactly. It opens truth into something better:

> . . . ritual
embouchure's loveliest utterances:

> myth,
> Myth and song.

[Dan Beachy-Quick]

A little bird told me,

"Eleontic Primordium, well, Ol' Moneybags was riding the train from Chicago to Mattoon, Illinois to give a reading at Eastern Illinois University on January 29, 2009. And he was reading *All the Names of the Lord: Lists, Mysticism, and Magic* (Chicago, 2008) by Valentina Izmirlieva. On page 70, she quotes from 'The 72 names of the Lord,' a false prayer from the Slavonic erotapocritical corpora that she calls 'the best documented list of the divine names' in the tradition. Among the names listed are Power, Strength, Word, *Sother*, *Pantocrator*, Garment, Blossom, Herb, Creator, Sabaoth, Intercessor, and, towards the end of the list: '*Eleon* [possibly from Heb., *Elion*, "the Most High" or from Gr., *Eleos*, 'Mercy.']'

O'Leary's first draft of the poem has Eleotic Primordium.
He changed it because he thought it sounded too much
like "Eliotic," and he didn't want anyone to suspect he was
invoking Old Possum. "So, Eleontic. Going instead for total
obscurity!"

[Billie Chernicoff]

Later that same evening . . . looked up "erotapocritical."
"Another genre of the Adamic text (apart from prayer,
narration, and lament) is the question-and-answer
erotapocritical apocryphal literature in the form of riddles and
solutions."

Here's that essay about lists:

[here, a vanished link]

Link is good for a week, if you don't get it before then, reach
out and I can send it to you.

Izmilieva is ref'd in the first paragraph. Peter wrote this around
the same time as *Phosphorescence* and he read it as part of the
celebration for the chapbook *Benedicite*.

[Devin King]

I'm still interested in "the foraging way" vs. "the wandering way," especially in terms of the recent discussion of doubt *qua* kerygma (or vice versa).

Steven, thanks for introducing "theologies of glory" vs. "theologies of the cross." Obviously I think Peter tips on the side of the first, although I wonder whether "the cross," for Peter, is the materialist vector or plane, in (as others have suggested) an almost purely Whitmanian sense. This would, for instance, inform, of not fully explain, the tension between Peter's use of recondite, abstract vocabulary and outright neologisms with his almost Clare-like consciousness of the material world (see the final poem in *Phosphorescence,* which I think is a stunner and out-Clares Clare). In other words I'm suggesting that the wood of Peter's particular cross really is wood, but the nails are language, the diaphanous freedom of language at every level. And the body? That remains a question to me (across Peter's work).

Re. "the scandal of Peter's lack of doubt," I think a very good answer is what Dan BQ offers here: "Peter's electric anaphora, in the rapid-fire insistence that each thing in the catalog is wholly its own unique shining forth and yet completely in relation to every other singular spark of existence itself." This is an amazing definition of Peter's very particular lack of doubt. And with that "shining forth" we also get, of course, the link to Hopkins. For Hopkins, the "shining forth" perhaps outshadows the "relation," but in Peter's work there is a co-illumination.

Part of me wants to dive into a deep and even giddy close reading of "Coda" (*Phosphorescence,* 65), but I will forbear.

On the doubt question, it seems to me that through doubt a set of possibilities—a range of poetics—become possible, and like all possibilities these exclude others. And that, in complement, through non-doubt (however defined), another, different set of possibilities (and therefore poetics) become possible, offer themselves. Praise is one form this non-doubt takes, although not the only one (dogma is another, and I would argue a meditative attention in the Weilian sense might be a third). And of course praise via cataloging, à la Smart.

I'm also very interested in how this conversation might, with a shifting of gears, apply to or bring into relation Peter Larkin's work. But Larkin's work may be my obsession alone? Larkin's attention to the natural world, his insistence on an abstract vocabulary of experience, and his quasi-resort to cataloging (a sort of cataloging at any rate) resonate here.

[G.C. Waldrep]

"Is the scandal of Peter's lack of doubt, in fact, far more scandalous than we thought? . . . Is there room in this poetry for sin, for the evident 'tragedy' of human life and history that would require the prodigious and interruptive event of the Incarnation of a God that is not continuous with but radically other than creation?"

Yes—this question has occurred to me vaguely but now snaps into focus. It's difficult to frame an objection to the lack of pain in someone's poetry—could you make it a bit sadder, scarier, angrier, please?—and yet there are those times, even with great writers and thinkers, like Emerson for instance, I find myself choking on the optimism; if there were a theologian of glory in "the American religion," I suppose Emerson would be it.

What distinguishes my experience of Peter's work is what I referred to above as its convulsive character. Perhaps there's a better way to describe this quality. The recognition that nature is earthshaking Poseidon, not just leafy Pan—that it is dangerous and that transformation—geologic, genetic, chemical, fleshly, spiritual—involves destruction as well as creation. And trauma, as Ovid knew.

Where is this in Peter's work? The density and velocity. Or just the work's intensity. Nothing this intense comes without danger. Danger, though, is not the same thing as tragedy (though it implies tragedy). Or suffering.

Someone like Messiaen might be interesting to think about: lots of birds, lots of Catholicism, lots of suffering.

*

Frye's book on Blake begins, as I recall (I don't have it with me) with a theory of mind according to which the "reality" of something is a function of how intensely it is perceived: so if I see the sun as a company of angels, I see it as "more real" than someone who sees it as a guinea (coin). This is because the metaphor of the angels is a greater leap, requiring / generating more energy, more intensity, than the metaphor of the coin. In a funny inversion of Pound, the imagination charges the symbol with reality. This is essentially a religious way of thinking.

Another way of assessing the reality of something is to ask not how intensely do I perceive it but rather: how much does it characterize ordinary life? This is how modernism tends to work (even down to today): the artist notices that some part of their experience is not represented in art and finds a place for it. Thematically and technically. Whatever it happens to be: handbills in Apollinaire, multiple perspectives in Picasso, movies in O'Hara, drugs in Ginsberg, etc. The extent to which apparently "stable" thought is the product of highly fluid and variable mental processes in Ashbery. The important thing, though, is that these things compel themselves into the poem not because of a particularly intense or privileged relationship to the poet, but because they occupy a significant part of the poet's experience and that of the culture at large.

If we're working with the religious, Frye model, as I think Peter fundamentally is, we can charge symbols with extraordinary power, but when we do so, everything turns into myth and metaphysics. This is what happened with "The Second Coming," originally a poem explicitly about the upheavals of the late 1910s. I would submit that that poem *couldn't* address politics directly even if it wanted to (though Yeats does so plenty of times elsewhere), due to its mythic intensity. You put something in a kiln, it's gonna get cooked.

But the problem with this model is that as it recognizes the seriousness of the political stakes in mythic terms, it turns politics into myth, and thereby makes politics inaccessible in its *own* terms. "Not men, but heads of the hydra" Duncan writes (again, I don't have the book, but I think it's in "The Multiversity") referring to the Berkeley administration and the powers behind the Vietnam War. The thing is, they *aren't* heads of the hydra—they are in fact men—and if you approach them as other than men, you have abdicated that fact, that part of reality. You may think, with Frye, that you've done so in order to enter into a higher reality, but then you may find out that you've simply entered a *different* reality, a more remote, more abstract reality.

        *

On the other hand (returning to Steven's contribution), I can't abandon secular skepticism (though I might characterize it differently). So many of the endeavors of the twentieth-century avant garde that Palmer elegizes in the talk I cited—Schoenberg, Picasso, Cage, Black Mountain poets, NY School poets, poststructuralism—have been about open form, drift, dissemination, multiplicity, the elimination of hierarchy. "My thought must be without sanction," Duncan writes in *The H.D. Book*. Christianity, on the other hand, *is* hierarchy. It always has to be the main thing; it can't *not* be the main thing, or else it isn't properly itself. Its authority cannot be checked or it loses all meaning. As a character puts it in a particularly wrenching moment in *Spotlight:* How do you say no to God?

In order to play any role in the culture whatsoever, poetry must retain the ability to say no. Even to God.

But in a monotheism, you have to subordinate yourself and all other values. And so the question remains: how is the poem's necessary errancy not trammeled by the act of proclamation and the *itinerarium mentis in deum?*

[Stephen Williams]

"In order to play any role in the culture whatsoever, poetry must retain the ability to say no. Even to God." This is a fascinating statement. But I'm with Celan on this one (yes/no).

I don't think these sorts of questions are ever either/or. But the position one takes opens a field of possibility, or possibilities—as I said. I'm interested in what the lack of doubt (if it be that) in Peter's poetics makes possible, and only in a residual way what (if anything) it precludes.

I might say the position itself constitutes a field. And Peter's, like Whitman's, is a field of admittance. Of course there is "subordination," because it is a poem, a text-artifact ordered in a certain way. What you call "the poem's necessary errancy" always constitutes a subordination of thought and/or experience (to language, first and foremost). This errancy is convoked within language, that is, within subordination. (Blake's essential sleight-of-hand, along with Whitman's, and perhaps even Mackey's, indeed all the "Orphic" poets', begin to persuade us that this isn't so.)

I like the idea that an objection frames a lack, just as a lack frames an objection. To proceed from your question of "intensity": is it the intensity that frames a lack, or the lack (of doubt, in this case) that frames Peter's intensity? (Asking for a friend—as they say—)

[G.C .Waldrep]

P.S. But I have to admit I've never believed in "ordinary life," as such. It's all extraordinary. And I do think all of Peter's work—especially the three books we're discussing—insists on this.

I believe that in order for the yes to really be a yes, a *true* yes, and for the no to be a true no, you have to go all the way down the paths those questions take . . .

G.C., I'm not sure I understand your question. What do you mean by "framing"? (Also, the friend?)

[Stephen Williams]

Was a jest. Apologies.

[G.C. Waldrep]

Re "ordinary life": hmmm, let me try to think about it this way. I think Peter's books, starting with this one, insist on the extraordinary life as a totality. And I think this is an act of will—evolving a long poem in a space absolutely (in the mathematical sense) defined by some conception of the "extraordinary" (which normally can only exist in a context established by the "ordinary"). Perhaps when we are speaking of the scandalous "lack of doubt" in Peter's work, what we are really talking about is the intensity of the will (bent to a particular end).

I've wondered (but never asked) whether this comes from, for instance, Blake's *Four Zoas*—although one could just as easily cite any poet who embraced the visionary long poem, from Milton to Duncan, Mackey, or some who are on this document.

The poem as the creation of a world (the world; any world).
Creation having no "doubt," only advents and recognitions.
In Peter's case, the creation of a world out of . . . the world:
grounded in a shared world but not limited to that world, in
any natural conception.

What this begs is a question of the role of the will (I am speaking
theologically, but also aesthetically). Is *Phosphorescence* a *willful*
poem? Or *Hidden Eyes*? (Not so sure about *Earth Is Best*.)

[G.C. Waldrep]

After I sent the previous I was thinking about Habit in Proust:
all that the brain reads as "ordinary," but then the web of habit
comes undone and that's the vision . . .

Regarding totality: it occurs to me that the involvement with
the solar eclipse, and the "path of totality," is a figure for a
totality that nonetheless, because it is always in process, holds
incompleteness within it. It's a way of having it both ways.

[Stephen Williams]

Soundtrack for this entry:
The Advisory Circle, "Learning Owl Reappears"

Some thoughts have concocted and condensed in my mind
of what I have seen walking about in midsummer eves and

I should not care if I got a few of the subjects on ivory now, to study upon with fresh recollections of similar appearances next midsummer if God spare me; I prefer doing them very small for they are not great things by themselves but wings, terraces or out buildings to the great edifice of the divine human form—otherwise snares. But I have beheld as in the spirit, such nooks, caught such glimpses of the perfumed and enchanted twilight—of natural midsummer, as well as, at some other times of day, other scenes, as passed thro' the intense purifying separating transmuting heat of the soul's infabulous alchemy, would divinely consist with the severe and stately port of the human, as with the moon thron'd among constellations, and varieties of lesser glories, the regal pomp and glistening brilliance and solemn attendance of her starry train.

—Samuel Palmer to George Richmond / Shoreham, Kent, Novr. 14, 1827

[Devin King]

⸻

"I wonder whether 'the cross', for Peter, is the materialist vector or plane, in (as others have suggested) an almost purely Whitmanian sense."

This is a helpful qualification, G.C. I am interested in the way Peter's acknowledgment of the pervasiveness of physical decay and entropy (ineradicable conditions of finite existence) might serve as de facto hamartiology in the trilogy; with a corresponding fungal soteriology, as we will later see in *Earth*

Is Best: the mushroom's quasi-Christological enfolding of death in life.

I suppose I was trying, with the glory/cross dichotomy, to establish Peter as doing something very different than, say, Fanny Howe, Geoffrey Hill, or Shane McCrae, fellow Christians but who seem particularly attuned to the pervasiveness of suffering, the oppressive weight of history and ancestral guilt, the inert density of language as a record of ignorance, violence, social injustice, our alienation from God, etc. These concerns don't seem to exercise Peter's poems. Cards on table: my own sympathies incline toward the "theology of glory" that I am imputing to Peter, but I am also sensitive to the challenges often leveled against this kind of cosmic optimism. Stephen gets to this, I think, with his great point about the danger of mythologizing and metaphysicalizing the historical and the political (Mackey, observing this same tendency in Duncan, called it "cosmologizing"). A certain dramatic or ironic distance from any particular instance of human suffering seems the inevitable outcome. I don't really know what to do with this, except to ask whether we can allow that to retain a town cosmologizer, preserving at least one mythic, ambivalent vantage over the whole, might itself have a positive political function?

Moneybags, paraphrasing monks in the film *Into Great Silence*:

> *If you abolish the symbols, then you tear down*
> *the walls of your own home.*
>
> *You should unfold the core of the symbols—*
> *We are the questions. (Phosphorescence, 32)*

*

"In order to play any role in the culture whatsoever, poetry must retain the ability to say no. Even to God."

Is poetry most "responsible" (in Duncan's sense, "to keep / the ability to respond") when it exercises the negative liberty of the unequivocal "no"?

I too am with Celan (and G.C.). For Augustine, we always say simultaneously "yes" and "no" to God. This is, in a nutshell, the doctrine of original sin. But there's also Julian of Norwich's nut, a little hazelnut her "shewing" placed in the palm of her hand:

> "What may this be?" And it was answered generally thus, "It is all that is made." I marveled how it might last, for I thought it might suddenly have fallen to nothing for littleness. And I was answered in my understanding: It lasts and ever shall, for God loves it. And so have all things their beginning by the love of God.

Being is interpenetrated with nothing, God's "yes" with our "no." She calls sin "behovely," despite but also, strangely, because of which "all shall be well and all shall be well and all manner of thing shall be well."

Arguably, it is only with the dawn of modernity, represented, say, in the philosophy of Descartes, that these kinds of paradox, the *lingua franca* of Christian mysticism and metaphysics, become intolerable and, eventually, unintelligible. The foundationalist obsession with "apodictic" certain knowledge ("justified true belief," etc.) about God or anything else for that matter, though certainly evident in much religious discourse today, is alien to the predominantly pre-modern religious thinkers Peter draws from (we haven't yet mentioned the significance of Dionysius the Areopagite).

Is it possible, despite the resolute anti-foundationalism that purportedly underpins the 20th century avant-garde, that a trace of this same bid for certainty remains, if only the certainty that reality reduces to the pure immanence of an aleatory chaosmos? The absolutes of drift and dispersal? How "open" is *that* field, really? Language poetry has always struck me as a species of positivism, and as such may be less of a swerve from than an intensification of the ethos of the New American Poetry. This is why Peter's work, as Billie, Stephen, and others have noted, is somewhat incongruous with the "experimental" canons of Modernism, despite his obvious affection for and indebtedness to them. His poetry suggests that immanence finds its peculiar integrity, its "openness," only in transcendence. "The poem's necessary errancy" is its condition of being a finite production, but the eschatological proviso ("all shall be well and all shall be well") perhaps qualifies what "errancy" means for a Peter as opposed to a Palmer.

> Do you really know where you are in this time and in
>   this space, actually?
> When sunlight
> shines through the blackness of space, it's black.
> But I can see it.
>
> It's not a hostile blackness. Welcome
> to the moon's sphere. You're in
> the influx. After passing nothing, you're in the presence
> of the moon.
>
> (*Phosphorescence,* 48)

Hierarchy is certainly relevant here; though I question whether the "hierarchy" that the NAP sought to eliminate is the same "hierarchy" that Peter's work affirms. Is the hierarchy of the Roman Catholic Church as we know it, which a great deal of current research suggests is effectively an early modern invention, a counter-Reformation consolidation of power actually modeled on the structure of the Baroque (secular) monarchy, the same as the Dionysian *hierarkhia*?

[Steven Toussaint]

Enchanting evensong, Devin. Peter's vespers poem (*Phosphorescence*, 39) is likewise meditative, with Trakl's sensual melancholy, all the blueness in the world. It goes on for a long while, lingering in twilight, steeped in death. No lack of suffering there, Stephen. And what about Bromios? (*Phosphorescence*, 54-59) No lack of danger, destruction, weirdness. Yet the fear and sorrow and ruin in this poetry are suffused with glory too. Everything participates in the luminous. G.C. raised the question of will, and there is a thoughtful willfulness here that gives itself over to revelation, to *knowing* without understanding, reconciles itself with mysteries that cannot be solved, magnifying the glory *and the rot* of a "lutrid" world that may not be worthy of it. Is that grace?

From *Phosphorescence*:

Vespers. The little stranger. November's destroyed era he's lost in.
A sacred grove's rotted branchwork, leprous walls enclosing.
Where the holy brother used to wander

sunk in the soft pulsations of his madness.

Lonely last gasps of the evening wind.
Bowed head in the gloom of the olive trees. That fading
image.

Seismic, the generation's worsening.
The gazer's eyes filling with the gold of his stars.
At this hour.

Evening. Bells—never again to sound out—fading.
Ruination of the black walls of the square.
Sound of the dead soldier called to prayer.

An angel. Bleached. Etiolated.
A son sets foot in the empty house of his father.

(Phosphorescence, 39-40)

[Billie Chernicoff]

Billie, I'm glad you've turned attention to the more sober
parts of the trilogy. These books aren't all ecstatic celebration.
I too was reminded of that menacing *Bacchae* section in
Phosphorescence:

My mother's betrayers. Her sisters: liars. Whores.
Of rumor. I've made them manic. Because of this. Stung their wits.
With agitation. Forced them. Into mountain wilderness.
Where they mince in farcical tatters—.

(Phosphorescence, 55)

Hidden Eyes, understandably, is an anxious and brooding book. Sadness pervades the Moon section where Peter reflects on his mother:

You're aware
even then
of her sorrow,
the simplex
of never having been sufficiently loved
by her own mother, a matter
she will always overcompensate for by loving you
into these complex entanglements, the very
mesh from which
you will build this illustrious temple
and whose design
you can never entirely contemplate
not even now, after all these years

(*Hidden Eyes*, 19)

There's the unremitting anger of Mars. And perhaps my favorite passage from *Hidden Eyes* is in Saturn:

You're limited, pilgrim. You'll
never become secure in your profession. That's a limit.
    You'll never
win wide acclaim. That's a limit. You'll never stop
working to earn your keep. That's a limit. You'll never
    unlink your emotional life
from the troubles of your home as a child.

(*Hidden Eyes*, 110)

Disappointment. Frustration. Resignation. There's real, relatable pain here and it's powerful. Maybe it isn't tragedy but it feels like Chekhov to me, a playwright who's more likely to bring me to tears than Sophocles.

[John Tipton, Saturn]

Beautifully put, John. And thank you Billie and John for highlighting these passages. The sheer number of tonal registers and key changes the poems can accommodate is staggering.

[Steven Toussaint]

A morning spent catching up with all that's been added, in Chicago, migration on, the May-green of leaves and yesterday's intermittent rain making the air its own spring greenness. All here more reverie than thought, more fantasia than insight.

Thinking of the yes/no & the either/or—feeling the strange despair of never being able to stay in the ambivalent both for as long as one would want, as one can't be on wing and in tree at the same time (though one can think of the opposite condition in the midst of occupying the other, dream or melancholy or both). Suspecting somehow that very difficulty—another iteration of it in Parmenides's is/is-not—as a version of the cross, the geometry, per Simone Weil, of pure contradiction. The absolute horizontal—the earthly insistence, bearer of gravity's pressure, the way in which the Kirtland warbler lives now only in its managed wild-not-wilderness, the Des Plaines river's human-managed, human-made banks, the crisis entering the *logos* of the ecological, which casts us back on the mind's shoals, the destruction of our efforts to know, the ruin of our made forms of care. But also the absolutely vertical, the call or summons (*kerugma*) that holds the highest sphere via vital tether to the lower, angel's ladder hinted at in the crepuscular (if we see with Blake's eyes), a human ladder, too, if every step up is also a step down, Heraclitus's "The road up is also the road down," Emerson's stairs on which, sometimes, he awakes to find himself . . . To find oneself on the cross and not get off by saying to oneself "yes" or "no," why is it Peter's work makes me think this is one of the fundamental encouragements?

Also, today, the birds. Imagining per one of the earliest conversations on Peter's language, the nouns of the catalog, the elementals. I can, in a certain light, see those nouns in their lists as birds roosting in a tree, and then the magnet in the blood demands flight, and they fly up and gather in their lines.

Also, today, the erotic. The "you *phallic thumb of love* / and you *thruster holding me tight* / you pressure in the uterine clutch, you glare of the rich palpitation, you proposition of sperm / you orchid boat and you winged serpent" in *Phosphorescence*. Remembering echoing passages in the Venus section of *Hidden Eyes*. Not creativity as the mark of poetic worth, but procreativity—the poem that is *worlding* rather than just *wording*.

[Dan Beachy-Quick]

In some respects this is a continuation of my earlier small thought, on the theophanic or presentational quality of Peter's syntax, and what others have said on the same or similar subjects (like Dan's observation that "each thing in the catalogue is wholly its own shining forth and yet completely in relation to every other singular spark of existence itself"). Like others, I'm struck by the forcefulness (the willfulness? the doubtlessness?) of Peter's vision and language—what Stephen Williams calls its "density and velocity." Indeed, it has a crushing, extrusive quality, and for this reason reminds me of lines from Hopkins's "God's Grandeur": "The world is charged with the grandeur of God. . . . / It gathers to a greatness, like the ooze of oil / Crushed." Today I'm thinking about the shining-forth that Peter performs in oily terms. His syntax crushes, pulverizes, releases lovely oil, performs a rite of unction or anointing.

An oil is a lipid, a fat. The decadence of Peter's language is a kind of "lavish flesh and savory inners," the slit glistening of hidden fullness, fulfillment. His books sizzle, to my nose, like "fragrant altars buttered with gleaming, oleoresinous fat." The river in *Phosphorescence* is a river of fat: it is "waxy in semiliquid aspic"; it is "warm and gelatine." Birds preen their wings with "fatty acids." The mushrooms in *Earth Is Best* are "rubbery-gelatinous" and "waxy lustrous / yellow and esculent." Consciousness is, like fat, an "overplus," an "excessive superfluity." The *noosphere* glistens from space like shook foil, like crushed oil.

The fatted calf is an offering. To Dan's thought there might be "something sacrificial in Peter's work"—yes. If consciousness is fatty, Peter presents thought as a lustrous, marbled "offering" at "thought's wooden table" (*Phosphorescence*, 62). And yet the mind is a bird—and, notably, the bird is "kept uncut" while the heifer, she-goat, and ram are each "split . . . up the middle," with the "halves" placed each "apart from the other" (*Phosphorescence*, 23, cf. "Covenant of the Pieces"). The unsplit bird reminds me, by contrast, of Dickinson's meditations on the split lark (cf. Dickinson, "Split the Lark"), a poem about doubt (Sceptic Thomas!) if there ever was one. The "bulb after bulb in silver rolled" that "gush" from the eviscerated lark are meager pearls of seed-fat, not music. Better, Dickinson suggests, to have kept its song unanalyzed, the inner flesh left undisplayed.

Some questions: is fat/oil the outcome of forcing it (splitting, crushing, enjambing the line) in lieu of faith? Consciousness is excessive; poetry is excessive, decadent. It shows the fat. Can it keep the faith?

Or is the poet precisely the bringer of a cut, a crisis (daring to eat peaches, etc.)—not the person of faith, but the church-militant, who comes to fulfill the faith, to force the oil to its final meridian?

[Kylan Rice]

———

A few thoughts, somewhat scattered I'm afraid. Sorry—grading!

G.C. and Steven, you'll recall I said that poetry must *retain* the ability to say No. This is entirely in keeping with Yes-No, since you can't have Yes-No without No.

As I see it, there really is no *equivocal* yes or no—an equivocal no is just a maybe.

When we talk about the "negative liberty of the unequivocal no," we're really talking about Satan, aren't we? Who's proved himself enduringly appealing to poets. But, if we assume that every no is unequivocal (at least at the moment it is uttered), we're really dealing with just the freedom that comes with saying no. Something like Dickinson's "No is the wildest word in the language" comes to mind. I'm okay with that as a model of responsibility.

"His poetry suggests that immanence finds its peculiar integrity, its 'openness', only in transcendence." Yes—this gets right at what animates Peter's work. But what about the requirement implicit in "only"? Doesn't that involve not a Yes-No, but a straight-up Yes?

I'm interested too, Steven, in your point about the history of the apodictic. But what about, on the one hand, Milton's attempt to "justify the ways of God to men"? Not premodern, but certainly a figure who looms large for Peter. And on the other hand, Thomas: why does he stick his finger into Jesus's wound? (Interestingly, etymonline suggests that "digitus" is cognate with "apodictic.")

Christianity admits a great deal of ambiguity about what's knowable and how. That's one of the most interesting things about it. But at a certain point the allegorical rubber has to meet the literal road, no? And that point (it would seem to me) is the Resurrection. It either happened or it didn't, correct? And once we acknowledge that, aren't we indeed engulfed in one vast either/or?

At what point is a paradox really a paradox, as opposed to a mere contradiction? It seems to me that a paradox is really a paradox only when you've arrived fully at the apparent "truth" of apparently incompatible realities. In other words, the ambivalent position, the negative capability position, seems to me only really itself, only really *true,* when it's arrived at as a last resort. (Is the same true of poetry itself?) Wittgenstein's *Tractatus* would be an example of this: you feel as though he's chewed through all the logic in the Western tradition, and only then, in section 7, does he arrive at the magnificent,

oracular utterance. Perhaps the progress through sections 1-6,
though, would be another measure of poetic responsibility.

[Stephen Williams]

Circling back to wade a little deeper into this passage near the
beginning of *Phosphorescence* . . .

We now begin our study of the mind
within. Let us use the words *psychic overtone*,
suffusion, or *fringe*.

Let us
speak in whispers of the one,
of the meticulous hinge
on the Book of Knowledge hidden in rapt

prelude. Apart. Come.

Let us use the word *re-entry*.
Let us sing the differentiating motions
whereby thought's signals
slide in runnels
down the mind's
great glacial expanse

pooling
at the base, lubricating
its massive shelves, its agonized
calves. Let us use
the word *epistrophe*

to mean the turning back of otherwise organized energy
to the supra-organized
diadem of the Godhead—premeditative acts
of prayer. Pre-

cognitive flights of birds.

(Phosphorescence, 5-6)

*

. . . hearing all the possibility concentrated in this summons:

prelude. Apart. Come.

First thought: Christ's *If any man come to me, and hate not his
father, and mother, and wife, and children, and brethren, and
sisters, yea, and his own life also, he cannot be my disciple.* For
the sake of revelation, the forsaking of the familiar, all you
know and love,

but I hear it too as *come apart*, fall apart, dis-integrate, cross
the threshold of the poem, enter the rite of the poem—
disintegration as a first stage of transformation, the prelude to
changing your mind,

or, the summoning of the poem by the poet, or of the poet by
the poem,

or, fairie! a beguiling, enchantment . . . *come away*, under the hill,

or, simply, *come in, come in, be a part of* this, whatever this
is or will be, a welcoming not only into the unknown of the
poem, but into a company, an "us," a *singing* us.

And there is the erotic resonance of "come." Well, isn't "prelude," at least etymologically, a synonym for foreplay?

And there's that "lubricating" oiliness Kylan brings to our awareness, thought chrism, overflowing.

[W]hereby thought's signals
slide in runnels
down the mind's
great glacial expanse

pooling
at the base, lubricating
its massive shelves, its agonized
calves.

Much verse that concerns itself with climate crisis is just not good poetry, because it has an agenda, knows beforehand what it wants to say—and the song gets lost in the program. But these slender, tense, musical lines that speak of "the mind's /great glacial expanse" and the glacier's "agonized calves," make of the earth and the mind one body, one magnificent, mysterious being. Those *calves* make me weep. A birth of consciousness.

"Epistrophe," the poem suggests, in response to catastrophe.

. . . the turning back of otherwise organized energy
to the supra-organized
diadem of the Godhead—premeditative acts
of prayer. Pre-

cognitive flights of birds.

*

None of this guesswork explains the poem, of course, and cannot communicate the experience of reading it. The poem remains an endlessly knowable secret, and on other days says other things.

. . . the meticulous hinge
on the Book of Knowledge hidden in rapt

prelude.

[Billie Chernicoff]

[Link to: Monk/Epistrophy]

I too must take some time to digest what went on over the weekend, while I was away. For now: it's good to return to *Earth Is Best,* especially after this recent reconnaissance with *Phosphorescence.* A few thoughts, for whatever they're worth:

1) I wonder whether in *Earth Is Best* the *impulse* to praise— the praise-vector—becomes reified, formalized, into a *structure* of praise (which the cycle's individual poem titles signal). The cataloging continues, but we're at a further point along some notional path. I don't mean "reified" in any pejorative way— rather diagnostically, as part of the impulse towards form.

2) Also thinking about what Peter calls "a *referential openness*" in his preface to *Earth Is Best.* This seems to embrace both

the cataloging and the praise-impulse, or praise-vector. And perhaps this is the manner in which Peter's work sidesteps the problem of assent, which, as we've seen, *kerygma* (as proclamation) (especially in a historically Christian sense) introduces. (Now seeing that you referenced this also, Steven)

3) Peter also in that preface alludes to "struggle," indeed "acute anxiety"—discordant notes in the praise-landscape his poems generally, but not always, occupy. It would be interesting to delve further into all three cycles in terms of these related dynamics. Certainly in *Earth Is Best* at least part of this "acute anxiety" is eco-anxiety (as per the Afterword), but . . . not all of it?

4) Peter's tendency towards neologism is wildly amplified in *Earth Is Best*. In terms of a notional Christian cosmology, there's a clue to this in "Ochre Vault": his contention that "obsolete praises are arguably a poetry of the resurrection" (60). (See also page 80, "a complete ecology of the resurrection.") I've long wished *Earth Is Best* did more with the resurrection trope than it does (if one views mycologies as a sort of life-beyond-death, and given the bread/meat/mushroom affinities). But maybe this would have seemed too easy, and/or too theologically predetermined?

5) And of course the apprehension of instress as a tool for the (re)mediation or repatriation of the extraordinary (in his thirty-third ode, aka, his lyric essay on Hopkins), by which we can only mean the ordinary perceived in registers of resonance and relation.

[G.C. Waldrep]

Not really meaning to get into a theological debate with Stephen, but I will add: the Thomasine tradition, as well as Christianity more generally, is unclear whether Thomas *did* in fact finger Christ's wound. The invitation and the response, in John 20, are both purely verbal—which is in its own right a fascinating concatenation, or collapse, of the physical with the verbal.

> And that point (it would seem to me) is the Resurrection. It either happened or it didn't, correct? And once we acknowledge that, aren't we indeed engulfed in one vast either/or?

Aha, but aren't we caught up in a Schrodinger's loop here? We are certainly engulfed in *something*. One way I read all of Peter's work, including the three texts we're discussing, is in terms of *ways of knowing*, different paths through the unknowing that knowing convokes or coerces. (Dan, I am thinking of your recent thinking about the poem on the page as an en-maze-ment, a structure or trace that renders the invisible maze visibly, if briefly.)

So, the attention (to the Greek roots of language or to birds) as one way of knowing; mycology in all its glorious weirdness as another way of knowing; astrology (coming right up!) as a third putative, notional way of knowing, of marking a path in that which engulfs us. I don't have to agree with, say, Peter's mycological or ornithological obsessions, or with any aspect of astrology, or for that matter with any underlying Christianity, to appreciate the three books as essays-in-knowing, utilizing modes of knowing. He could have used particle physics, Tarot, color theory, etc.

And yes to this:

> Much verse that concerns itself with climate crisis is
> just not good poetry, because it has an agenda, knows
> beforehand what it wants to say — and the song
> gets lost in the program. But these slender, tense,
> musical lines that speak of "the mind's / great glacial
> expanse" and the glacier's "agonized / calves," make of
> the earth and the mind one body, one magnificent,
> mysterious being. Those *calves* make me weep. A birth
> of consciousness.

I think Peter's "agenda" is affirmation, and I think he means it,
on any or every conceivable level. This might also explain, or
underpin, the lack of "doubt." A question: We're accustomed,
in our postmodern 21st-century way, to critique being an
inherent aspect of doubt. But can critique be an inherent part
of affirmation? Does anyone see critique as an aspect of either
Phosphorescence or *Earth Is Best*?

[still G.C. Waldrep]

Something I wanted to bring up a bit ago but managed not to:

We've mentioned the relative-clause-without-relative pronoun
form (of which the third line below is another example),
where the parts of the sentence suddenly snap together into
sense when the syntactic relationships become clear. Two
other regular features of the language seem worth mentioning.
(Forgive me if I've overlooked a comment that addresses
these.) The first is the use of repetitions such as:

Let the earth riot with a riot of living forms tithing
the tithe of the earth in tumults, in its theotrophous
     abundances
secret springtime ceremonies augur.

(Earth Is Best, 35)

I'm trying to remember something Peter said once about how, in this passage and others like it, he adapts the repetitive formula ("riot with a riot"; "tithing the tithe") from the *Zohar.* Later in the same poem there's the "Tree of Life radiating life" (36) and "Life that shines, shining forth" (37). In some cases there are subtle differences between the two instances of the word: I take there to be a difference between shining and shining forth, for example. Or life and Life. (Maybe that one's not so subtle.) Other times, it's less clear. Anyway, this feature of the work interests me. The reiterations convey little to no semantic meaning—but what does it do?

Second: the use of the possessive. If we look ahead to *Hidden Eyes* page 3 (though it occurs throughout the poetry), of the ten "Masters of Time," seven are ascribed to some specific power: "thaumaturgy's archangelic quicksilver"; "passion's volcanic principality"; etc. He uses the apostrophe-s version of the possessive rather than the "of" version out of, I'm almost certain, a Poundian desire for *condensare.* But then why bother with the possessive in the first place? I don't know but I feel as though there's a ceding of something going on, so that "dominion's lordly fortunes" always implicitly means "*not my* lordly fortunes," "the Sun's stunning magicum" means "*not my* stunning magicum," etc. A version of Duncan's "that is not mine." Interesting, if true, that such a gesture of humility should take place within this bombastic, fanfare-like passage, and that he should return to it so frequently.

[Stephen Williams]

Earth Is Best holds many of my favorite of Peter's poems. "First Amanita Ode" has a place, for me, beside Lorine Niedecker's "Lake Superior" as a poem that characterizes the region, a great North Central poem. This book catches the joys of foraging, of discovery, like few works I know, through the little intensities of warblers and mushrooms (and rare words). Their interconnectedness (or ecologies) are figures for intelligence. Yet it's a book of lament as well as praise, the pleasures evanescent at the moment of discovery, "True nature. Shining through. / Even in the closing season." I think of Albert York's response, when asked why he paints: "I think we live in a paradise, this is a Garden of Eden, really it is. It might be the only paradise we ever know, and it's just so beautiful, with the trees and everything here, and you feel you want to paint it. Put it into a design."

[Devin Johnston]

Agreed that many of my favorite individual poems of Peter's are in *Earth Is Best*. The shorter odes in particular (not to be confused with Peter's "Tatters," of which there are also a few in *Earth Is Best*). But the poems I keep returning to in *Earth*

Is Best are the four longer, non-ode poems that interrupt the main sequence: "The Dogs," "Ochre Vault," "Hidden Stone," and "Greenshine." "The Dogs" and "Ochre Vault" are simply magnificent. I am still not quite sure how they work, but I keep returning to them. (I am a slow thinker when it comes to analyzing poems I love. I return to them again and again across many years and only gradually accrue "ideas" about them.)

In general I admire the way Peter reinterrogates (or reintegrates) formal concerns anew with each new ode. Part of the readerly pleasure of *Earth Is Best* is encountering each new ode on its own ground, sticking within the idiom and the mycological focus while re/investing that focus in formally fresh ways.

[G.C. Waldrep]

I finished *Phosphorescence* yesterday, and started *Earth Is Best* while pedaling my feet in circles on a stationary bike—letting my new hip get the little exercise it's allowed. I mention it only because the idea or the act of *repair* feels so prevalent in the vision spanning both volumes, a song whose inner dynamics are so built of the breath or *pneuma* that courses through all cosmos that to arrive at the Ode as primary form isn't only to praise, but to repair the world via that praise.

I find myself so struck by the wren as truest hero in *Phosphorescence*. The gathering of birds, the ornithomachy, on pages 53-54. The wren's defeat of the eagle:

Now here's the thing: the eagle is life itself, its

striving vital force always upward gaining,
always finally tiring. So what's the wren? The mind's
     feeling force–
the heavenly starlight that shines unwaning.

The body tires; the song is eternal.

*

& to *Earth Is Best*, feeling a difference in how the language is
behaving in the Odes. I feel less of the stunning tonal shifts
mentioned earlier, not that the verse is any less stunning. I
feel less of the poetry cycling through numerous iterations—
catalog, litany, anaphora, etc.—as if wandering through a
history of poetic utterance and the possibilities inherent
therein. In some sense, *Earth Is Best* is an arrival at a form that
can hold all it needs to hold—maybe the "Wren./Omen."
Coda that ends *Phosphorescence* is the wren's very song, the ode
that opens up the vocal possibility of the next book. & the
language in these Odes feels to me so astonishingly intricate
in its inner sonics. I feel Hopkins as a precedent, but not
only in sound and the suggestion of a sprung rhythm. More,
I feel in the poems an insistence that the poem itself is a
demonstration of the forces it's attending to—that one could
almost draws lines connecting (thinking here of the Fourth
Ode in particular) linking sound to sound and find that one
has drawn a map of the mycelium itself . . . as if the sonics are
themselves a living matter, a fungal matter, spoor-stuff, and
the music of the language itself is one of the forces that takes
what's dead, and turns it back to life's own fecund loam.

[Dan Beachy-Quick]

Hello all,

It's been a very busy and intermittently rough few weeks for me, as some of you here know, and I've been kicking myself because I have not been able to read this as it unscrolls before me, catching it only in bits and snatches. Nor have I been able to give the books themselves the time they deserve. So at the risk of doubling back and repeating (repetition—always a sign of the uncanny!), I would like to emphasize two related concepts which have arisen in our discussion: (1) the transgression of religious poetry under our current and longstanding secular conditions—a powerful sign, if you will, of the transgression of the sacred in general; and (2) Peter's poetry as sacrificial, which I hold to be true, if not often that obvious.

Regarding (1): That simple, shocking moment early in *Phosphorescence* when, after some pages of avian and cherubic lyricism, we get the statement "God made this, composed it" (8). Well yes, Peter, we pretty much figured out that's what you believe, but the *statement* is crucial, it carries great verbal force, given the extravagance of what comes before and after (and immediately after comes what I take to be a wild midrash on Genesis, with science, both archaic and modern, providing terms for a "maelstrom" of creative force). Whether you believe or not, the door is opened to wonder; we see Nature and human life anew. Peter quotes Oppen's "shipwreck of the singular" (9) and then claims a "*Rebeginning.*" This is important, because Oppen is one of our greatest secular poets, a Marxist, but one who refers constantly to the "metaphysical." From which, of course, we cannot escape.

Regarding (2): at the end of that amazing riff on Abraham and the "thick and dazzling darkness" (Peter is utterly possessed by that episode), he asks, rhetorically, "And what kind of god requires all this sacrifice from us?" (*Phosphorescence*, 24) A mysterious god, unknowable, but ineluctably demanding. A god who insists upon language, more and more language, enormous excrescences and hyperbolic explosions of language. The shaman-poet must exhaust himself, bringing forth litanies (see pages 27-32) and giving himself entirely to this worship. Whitman, obviously, comes to Peter's aid again and again in this effort. Because ecstasy is hard work, sacrificial labor of the greatest intensity.

And I would note that when Peter, years later, gets more personal, as in the Moon and Saturn sections of *The Hidden Eyes of Things* (I refer you to my review), the comparatively (only comparatively!) simpler discourse is even more "sacrificial" because less extravagantly defended, in both the rhetorical and psychoanalytical senses. I hope we get into discussion of this book soon.

[Norman Finkelstein, Cincinnati]

Really happy now to be thinking about "extravagant defense," a poetics of extravagant defense. In terms of Peter's work, yes, but also in terms of many other poets whose work I love (e.g. Char, Celan). Thank you!

[G.C. Waldrep]

"A poet of sympathy," Patrick said earlier. Parsifal asking *what ails thee* of the earth itself, even of the cosmos.

Guided by Virgil, Dante tempers his sympathy. Peter feels the plight of being—tenderly, radically, anxiously, intemperately, a cosmologizer without distance or irony. A wren's euphoria.

An agenda of "affirmation." (G.C.) The lack of doubt in this poetry as a consequence of its devotion to what happens, affinity with what is, a *friendliness,* open-mindedness as a spiritual discipline.

Communion as the embrace of paradox, a commitment to it—Whitman's commitment, Blake's. The poet contradicts himself. The cosmos contradicts itself. God. They *seem* to. Peter's poetry teaches staying with it, till we are past seeming. "A fundamental encouragement," Dan called it.

Dan's comment about staying on the cross haunts me. Christ nailed to the tree. Odin hanging from it. Buddha sitting under the tree, not budging, staying.

The endless profusion of wor(l)ds, litanies. Wittgenstein's silence.

. . . The world

is both good and evil and yet neither, the matrix
of all possibilities. The *Gloria mundi* quarried
in primordial foretime was a bitter salt, mostly
black and evil smelling. The spirit
of chaos cannot be distinguished from the Holy Spirit.

Visionary gleam.
Clarity.

> —The Twenty-fifth Amanita Ode, Corruption.
> *(Earth Is Best, 63)*

I've been puzzling for a while over the violence of Acteon's doom, in "The Dogs" in *Earth Is Best,* and its relationship to the Bromios/Dionysus aria in *Phosphorescence of Thought*, wondering what these dark, charismatic, thrilling, frightening ancients are doing in this Catholic theology of glory. Now, reading again through the collective commentary, including your recent, Norman, I'm thinking about those appearances in the context of the hard labor of ecstasy, the ordeal of initiation, the sacrifice vision demands: Dionysus as the patron saint of the visionary. His followers must lose their minds. And Acteon, torn apart (*Apart. Come.*) for the sake of a glimpse of God, for the sake of "a new unanticipated thought."

[Billie Chernicoff]

Who, What, Where, When

Not:

Why or How
In Peter we come back to

Deixis

Again & again.

[Thomas Meyer]

G.C. responding to Thomas Meyer: yes, all three of these books seem to me to be extended, sustained exercises in deixis, that Franciscan element (although it could be construed otherwise). It's tempting to hazard that Peter puts the *Deus* into deixis, but I will leave more sober Greek etymologies to Dan et al.

One could also say that across this trilogy, the "who. What. Where. When" *is* the how.

To Billie, re the myth of Actaeon: I've been fascinated, not to mention repulsed, by this myth since I first encountered it as an adolescent. And "The Dogs" certainly interrupts *Earth Is Best,* flagrantly (I want to say "extravagantly," since we were using that word earlier). Its violence is shocking, and I, too, have puzzled over the function of this violence in *Earth Is Best.* But I think you may get it exactly right. I would be very interested in others' thoughts on how that poem functions in *Earth Is Best.*

[G.C. Waldrep]

The perceptions and experiences present in Peter's three books remained (and remain) alive and multidimensional upon re-reading. Thanks for everyone's thoughts and attention. I look forward to seeing everyone tomorrow.

The depth and reach of sound and lexicon feel boundless here, the Divine deeply present. Lacking any kind of Christian framework (I was expelled from the confirmation class held at the Episcopal church across the street) here are some random thoughts, alternative frames, from Way East of Suez.

The Christian/Catholic (and Islamic) world has God at its center, the Creator. "God made this, composed it." (*Phosphorescence*, 8, see Norm's entry, above). This has always felt like a *centripetal* world: everything, every gorgeous or horrible connected thing, leads back to God. As the Islamic mystics have it, the world and its attributes were created by God (including man) in order for God to see Himself. Infinite self-reflections of the Divine. Clouds, birds, feelings of love, despair, mushrooms, wine.

The monotheistic religions, even in their most gnostic forms, have never offered me access to the (largely familiar, I confess) experiences of enlargement and ecstasy and transcendence present in these books. So, I think I just skipped over references to God here, maybe reading the books I wanted rather than the ones Peter wrote. I believe this is not really what one is looking for in a literary critic, maybe it's what you want in a lawyer. It might possibly be a useful way into the work for Canadian readers, Emily?

In contrast to the monotheistic (and patriarchal) religions, the South Asian and Himalayan religions have always felt creative, myriad, welcoming, *centrifugal*: a central divine essence spins outward into shifting and colorful theogonies of deities, demons, spirits, enchanted beings and geographies. As Peter writes:

> *"This is the song of the hidden stone possessing a thousand forms."* (*Earth Is Best*, 45)

And surely the mycelium is Indra's Net (cf. *Atharva Veda*, § 8.8.8)?

> *"Far away in the heavenly abode of the great god Indra, there is a wonderful net which has been hung by some cunning artificer in such a manner that it stretches out indefinitely in all directions. In accordance with the extravagant tastes of deities, the artificer has hung a single glittering jewel at the net's every node, and since the net itself is infinite in dimension, the jewels are infinite in number. There hang the jewels, glittering like stars of the first magnitude, a wonderful sight to behold. If we now arbitrarily select one of these jewels for inspection and look closely at it, we will discover that in its polished surface there are reflected all the other jewels in the net, infinite in number. Not only that, but each of the jewels reflected in this one jewel is also reflecting all the other jewels, so that the process of reflection is infinite."*
>
> —*Francis H. Cook*, Hua-yen Buddhism: The Jewel Net of Indra

In a Zen-inflected world, the phenomena that illustrate "God's grandeur" make up the fabulous web of illusory phenomena that gives rise to dualistic (I/not-I, subject/object) thinking and distract us from the transcendent absence at the core of things.

And when we get to *Hidden Eyes*, Vedic astrology has some hidden planets that sometimes eat the others.

[Elizabeth T. Gray, Jr., New York City]

This easterly breeze is so fresh, Liz, Indra's net trembling in it.

Etel Adnan says, "it's not the poet who's the poet, it's the reader."

Rereading Thirty-third Amanita Ode, PARMENIDES/ CLOUDS, thinking about Indra's Net, and DEIXIS:

As clouds of air are transient showings of *instress* and *uplift*, clods of earth are slow-moving bodyings forth of *outlease* and *downspread*, antonymic twins.
As clouds are to the sky, so clods—especially in the form of mushrooms—are to the earth.
Instress and outlease, uplift and downspread describe the total planetary energetic system, integrating and unintegrating their appearances. And language is the field of manifestation. (*Earth Is Best*, 90)

[Billie Chernicoff]

Two thousand years after Parmenides declared that "thinking and being are the same," Descartes reframed the proposition into an inferential relationship. While his skeptical idealism has come in and out of fashion, his mapping of geometry to the abstract notation of algebra has not. All of modernity is downstream from his discovery of the isomorphism between algebra and geometry. Sometimes it's easier to picture a problem and sometimes it's easier to move symbols around. Cartesian coordinates allow you to switch back and forth. This mapping is the main move in mathematics: find a mapping, picture a problem in one structure and then solve a seemingly intractable problem in another structure.

Pete explicitly states that this is what he is doing in his trilogy on consciousness: birds, mushrooms, and astrology are mapped to the evolution of consciousness, altered states, and the unconscious, respectively. Obviously, he's not doing math, but it's a way to think about the structural relationships he sets up in these books, which is not the same thing as allegory. In "To the Public" at the beginning of *Earth Is Best,* he writes, "Poetry is a *referential openness* . . ." It is a representation in the modern sense. But unlike algebraic geometry, the movement in Pete's poetry is from one structure to another. Poets traffic mostly in metaphor, whether explicitly or not, but few to the degree that Pete does in his love of schema, classification, celestial hierarchies, etc. It allows him to immerse himself in one structure while obliquely uncovering reefs of consciousness. In that sense, his poetry is totally against positivism: he is always talking about what we can't talk about and he does it through mapping. The Thirty-third Amanita Ode *Parmenides/Clouds* is an almost complete depiction of this process from the initial essay about Parmenides and Hopkins to the Cloud/Clod weirdness at the end. Sometimes I forget how close he is to Hopkins.

Somewhat unrelated, Pete writes on page 19 of *Phosphorescence of Thought*, "For t*he language of God has no grammar; it consists only of name*s." Are the italics from a quote? I'm struck in re-reading these books that if not for the influence of Whitman, there would be no verbs in his poetry.

[Michael O'Leary, Chicago]

Now I must
110   teach of things

known without sight.
First, the wind
on the ocean,
waves, then ships,
115   pushed with hurricanes

that uproot trees
and erode mountains
with leveling sound.
Invisible wind exists,
120   see its destruction,

similar to water.
Both flood, overwhelm.
Rain's nasty combine.
Wind is as
125   real as water.

Every thing smells.
Why, then, can't
smells be seen?
Heat hurts, dude.
130   Cold's the worst.

I love music.
I can't see
any of these,
but they touch
135   me, and touch

is material, bodily.
In California, clothes
left outside become
damp. New Mexico:
140   they become dry.

Tell me you
see this happen!
You can't. Only
the fatal result.
145   Particles are small.

After years rings
wear, rocks are
hollowed by water
and a statue's
150   foot, luckily touched,

becomes a club.
All matter changes,
even if we
don't witness change.
155   Finally, things grow.

What unseen material
addition turns children
into adults, adults
into corpses? Bodies.
160   Things. We grow

from accumulation and
die by losing.
What? Who knows.
Yet we cannot
165   hold all things.

Space exists. Keep
void in mind.
You won't wander.
Without emptiness things
170   will not move.

Bodies stop bodies,
things aren't empty,
nothing moves without
nothing, void is
175   because we see

so much movement:
land, sea, heaven,
all have void.
Without it: one
180   massive packed glob.

Nothing is so
solid without void:
cave walls cry,
animals eat food,
185   trees grow, grow

fruit everywhere, I
hear sound everywhere,
around corners and
through walls and
190   cold goes inside.

These need void.
Last: same size,
different mass. Hold
an egg in
195   your hand. In

the other, an
egg sized stone.
One's void surpasses.
It's so clear,
200   the void exists.

The entire universe
is two things:
body and void.
Anything else is
205   them or property

or accident.

Lucretius, Book One

[Devin King]

Inscape. Instress and uplift. Good to remember to exercise the
other senses in this time of the sovereignty of the eye.

This translation is wonderfully distilled, musical, really a
pleasure. Giving myself a crash course on the mystery of
substance and accidents for the Greeks and in the Church, but
you and Lucretius teach it best here, Devin.

"Mycopoetic euphoria is effervescent foraging: in language,
in dictionaries, in ideas, in old poems, in the poems of
the future. It is a pursuit of uncultivated wildness at
once restorative (because adept at destroying toxins) and
entheogenic, awaking divine awarenesses within."
(Earth Is Best, 103)

A poetics of resurrection.

[Billie Chernicoff]

Love that three-word line, Devin. But you know I'm a sucker for it.

[John Tipton]

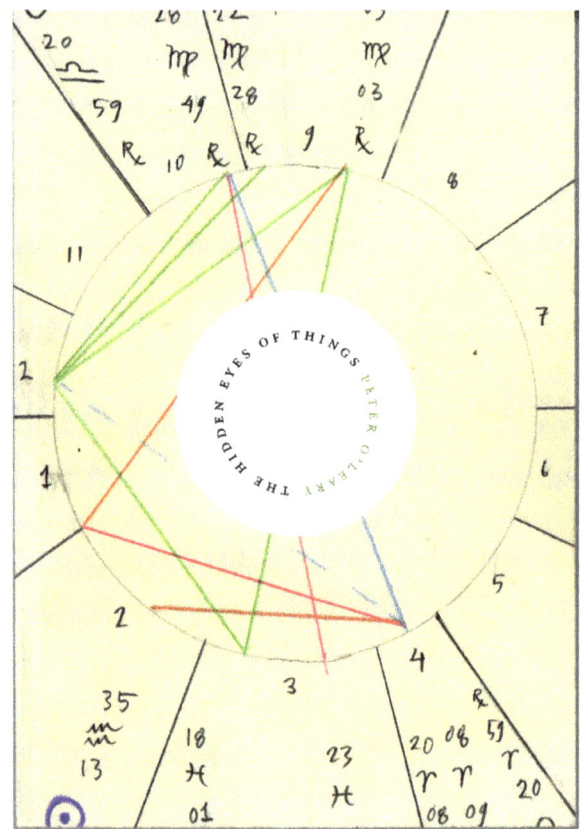

Michael: What distinguishes Peter's Descartes-like transpositions from allegory?

Reading Peter's work I am sometimes put in mind of Angus Fletcher's *Allegory: The Theory of a Symbolic Mode,* in which he argues (despite his subtitle) for a psychological rather than a symbolic notion of allegory:

> We find that [the allegorical hero] conforms to the type of behavior manifested by people who are thought (however unscientifically) to be possessed by a daemon. This notion may be hard to accept, but only because the present common idea of a daemon is of a wild, unkempt, bestial, monstrous, diabolic creature, whereas ancient myth and religion recognized many mild and benificent daemons, the *eudaimoniai.* [. . .] Daemons, as I shall define them, share this major characteristic of allegorical agents, the fact that they compartmentalize function. If we were to meet an allegorical character in real life, we would say of him that he is obsessed by only one idea, or that he has an absolutely one-track mind, or that his life was patterned according to absolutely rigid habits from which he never allowed himself to vary. It would seem that he was driven by some hidden, private force . . .

So, allegory as "an immensely pervasive strain of demonism" (*Earth Is Best*, 43).

Initially I found this idea difficult to accept, not for the reason Fletcher cites but because he makes too large a claim, I felt, for the dynamism and aliveness—the substance—of allegorical figures. It seemed like the kind of move one makes because it's interesting, not because it's true.

But with *Hidden Eyes* it all seemed to make a kind of sense: the possession, the grip, of one thing by another rather than (or in addition to) a more abstract notion of "correspondence." Why *Hidden Eyes*? I think I only read Fletcher after the other volumes had appeared.

What does the psychological notion of allegory permit that the conventional, symbolic notion does not? The occult property of the "hidden, private force." But also, allegory's "demonism" allows the figure to be at once totally possessed ("one-track mind") and at the same time active: compartmentalized *function* rather than restricted reference. Like the idea (figure) of the "path of totality," which combines the totality of the eclipse with the necessary incompleteness of anything in motion, anything that's "on the way."

[Stephen Williams]

I learned from the only dude in Wicker Park who could teach it, John! Thanks for the kudos friends—I hope the Lucretius helped emphasize and re-direct Michael's point.

Also, *Hidden Eyes* is probably the only book ever written that could faithfully be compared to *Future*, the last LP of Sinatra's *Trilogy*, a kind of Scott Walker-style concept record where Sinatra travels on a spaceship to each planet:

[See:] "What Time Does the Next Miracle Leave?"

[Devin King]

Coming back late to the conversation on Actaeon, the trouble of that violence, and the undergirding mythic lore of Orpheus and Dionysis—the strange way that underneath the resurrection of Christ-as-God we have also, across the whole trilogy, the mythos of the pantheon. I love it deeply that the Christian and the Pagan refuse to cancel each other out, nor do I sense in Peter's work any simple exegesis that gives one priority or claim over the other, despite the poet's faith so abundant on the page. It is as if these varying conceptions of God and gods are themselves part of the penetralium that consciousness itself is—the mind pierced by the history of realities that have claimed for themselves a portion of the actual.

I've gone back to Jane Ellen Harrison's *A Prolegomena for the Study of Greek Religion*, where she speaks of the "arduous effort after holiness." She writes of a brutal rite in which men daubed in gypsum tear apart and eat a bull—one of the manifestations of Dionysus, as Bromius:

> But nothing, nothing, no savage rite, no learned mythological confusion, daunts the man bent on edification, the pious Orphic. The task of spiritualizing the white-clay-mei, the dismembered bull, was a hard one, but the Orphic thinker was equal to it. He has not only taken part in an absurd and savage rite, he has brooded over the real problems of man and nature. There is evil in the universe, human evil to which as yet he does not give the name of sin, for he is not engaged with problems of free-will, but something evil, something that mixes with and mars the good of life, and he has long called it impurity.

His old religion has taught him about ceremonial cleansings and has brought him, through conceptions like the Keres, very near to some crude notion of spiritual evil. The religion of Dionysos has forced him to take a momentous step. It has taught him not only what he knew before that he can rid himself of impurity, but also that he can become a Bacchos, become divine. He seems darkly to see how it all came about, and how the old and the new work together. His forefathers, the Titans, though they were but 'dust and ashes,' dismembered and ate the god; they did evil, and good came of it; they had to be punished, slain with thunderbolts; but even in their ashes lived some spark of the divine; that is why he their descendant can himself become Bacchos. From these ashes he himself has sprung. It is only a little hope; there is all the element of dust and ashes from which he must cleanse himself; it will be very hard, but he goes back with fresh zeal to the ancient rite, to eat the bull-god afresh, renewing the divine within him.

A violence that is a form of ascent—it's an economy the modern self shuns in near horror, but an economy our ancient selves recognized as one of nature's fundamental patterns. In Actaeon we have a demonstration not only of the goddess's cruelty, but a vision of reciprocity's fundamental law: that the hunter becomes the hunted, that you must suffer as you make suffer. All of this seems to speak to me of wild, almost unimaginable *one-ness* of the world, which may be the mystic's dearest thought, that all is one, I sense such a thought in Peter's work. But *oneness* is a hard thing.

[Dan Beachy-Quick]

"a wild, almost unimaginable *one-ness* of the world." I've been finding my way to something like that too, Dan. This poetry knows the old gods are still here, in the sky and in our psyches—in our language, resurrected as we speak. In the cosmology of the Trilogy, each sacrifice or revelation recalls or heralds another, just as Liz describes the infinite mirroring of Indra's net, just as the seeds of all syllables are contained in Om.

> . . . *Ego sum alpha et omega, principium et finis*—
> for revelation is an alphabetic, an
> exegetical totality . . . (*Hidden Eyes*, 25)

and

> Vespertine Venus, eophoric flame, rival of Sun and
>   Moon, alone
> among the stars shining with such brilliance
> whose rays cast a shadow, auguring
> the almighty Lord of the world:
> Love. (48)

and

> Allegorize what fades from view.
> Manifest the inadequate.
> Enact the shapeless.
> Follow the goddess. (130)

Not "a" goddess, *the* goddess.

There's an at-oneness, too, in the multiplicity of the speakers of *Hidden Eyes*—the Orphic scientist, geeky astrologer— Pythagoras, Jung, Freud, Ronald Johnson, others—the poet's Virgils and Beatrices, teachers and companions—their systems, voices, in harmony, a shared authority.

Hidden Eyes can be terrifying in its embrace of what is. The apocalypse has already happened, the battle is raging in heaven.

But then there's this, from the coda (and the wonder throughout, the love throughout).

> You learned that the Earth, beaten and betrayed, is
>   brighter than any star, better than any fate,
>   more epic than any autobiography, more
>   sympathetic than any magic. (170)

*

And this, from "At the Gates of Delirium" is so radical:

You learned the aspect and the transit, all the melancholy
houses, the eminence and the intermediaries, the seasons and
the sidereal gods, the vault and the myth,
the sublunary daemonism imbuing the silver-blue light
with texture and shadow. How do you know
any of these things are true?

Feeling.

How?

The eophanic visionary reality of the dawn world
beamed into this world through feeling.

What can be seen in
other worlds through seercraft or star lore can be felt
in this world
in premonitions or
starry prescience.

This

you learned in righteous onrush and
sacred drudgery both. An ongoing commitment, a
long song convergence, a
liturgical ambush. (118)

*

Feeling = knowing. I was not expecting that any more than the
goddess.

[Billie Chernicoff]

Stephen Williams: Regarding the distinction between allegory
and what Pete is doing. Thinking about it now, maybe there
isn't a huge difference. But I'm struck by the degree to which
Pete is not concerned with the precision of the mapping
of, say, the unconscious to astronomy. He stakes the claim
and then uses it as a vehicle for discovery. The mapping is
generative in a way that allegory is not. Even when he was
discussing the Mars section during the Zoom call last week,

he detailed the challenge of working through it. He had no idea about Mars and the unconscious before getting to that section; the schema led him to uncover the martial aspects of the unconscious. The key to Descartes' discovery is the isomorphism between algebra and geometry, which strikes me as allegorical. Pete's move is more epimorphic or one-directional. He doesn't look back. Our job as readers is to intimate the relations.

This one is largely for Devin, Ox, [See:] "Solar System (Remastered 2000)"

I know that Pete is not a huge B. Wilson fan, but the lyrics are worth quoting in full:

What do the planets mean? And have you ever seen
Sunrise in the morn? It shined when you were born.
Saturn has rings all around it
I searched the sky and I found it

Solar system
Brings us wisdom

Then there's the Milky Way, that's where the angels play
You've seen the lover's moon, looks good in the month of June
Neptune is god of the sea-ea-ea
Pluto is too far to see

The constellations are stars that form animals
Leo and Capricorn, too
Star bright, star light
Make this wish come true tonight

If Mars had life on it I might find my wife on it
Venus the goddess of love can thank all the stars above
Mercury's close to the sun
You'll see it when day is done

Solar

[Michael O'Leary]

Maybe these poems give us more doubt or "no" than we even
know what to do with. It is in Peter's involvement in things
like astrology, incantations, and so on. In the Catechism of the
Catholic Church: "All forms of divination are to be rejected:
recourse to Satan or demons, conjuring up the dead or other
practices falsely supposed to 'unveil' the future. Consulting
horoscopes, astrology, palm reading, interpretation of omens
and lots, the phenomena of clairvoyance, and recourse to
mediums all conceal a desire for power over time, history, and,
in the last analysis, other human beings, as well as a wish to
conciliate hidden powers. They contradict the honor, respect,
and loving fear that we owe to God alone" (CCC 2116).

And then: "All practices of *magic* or *sorcery*, by which one
attempts to tame occult powers, so as to place them at one's
service and have a supernatural power over others—even if this
were for the sake of restoring their health—are gravely contrary
to the virtue of religion. These practices are even more to be
condemned when accompanied by the intention of harming
someone, or when they have recourse to the intervention of
demons. Wearing charms is also reprehensible. *Spiritism* often

implies divination or magical practices; the Church for her part warns the faithful against it. Recourse to so-called traditional cures does not justify either the invocation of evil powers or the exploitation of another's credulity" (CCC 2117).

I don't mean to get so heavy-duty. But it's important stuff. Peter knows what he's doing. I mean that he knows the Catechism.

[Emily Tristan Jones]

Emily points to an aspect of what has always disturbed me about Peter's astrology project, that he and I have discussed many times. A distinction that could be drawn is between astrology-as-divination, per the passage Emily just quoted, and astrology as, in effect, a way of knowing: a fictive way, but a way of knowing nevertheless. What is possible through the way of knowing that astrology represents, that isn't possible any other way? (The same could be said for other occult and/ or gnostic practices, cf. Böhme's take on alchemy.)

Cartography is also a way of knowing, and also at least partly fictive, therefore at least partly occult, although as far as I know no church has banned maps or mapping yet. I read *Hidden Eyes* most charitably when I think of it as a mapping, a map—rather like Joseph Gordon Macleod's *Ecliptic,* which I presume stands behind *Hidden Eyes,* since Peter directed me to it many years ago. But I have to admit a very personal, and theologically-grounded, resistance to *Hidden Eyes* that I didn't have (except perhaps in patches) with *Phosphorescence* or *Earth Is Best.*

(I would cite Liz's *Salient* as an example of a deeply occult, but also historically specific and astonishingly informed, cartography of knowing.)

To take a further step back in the conversation: "A violence that is a form [of] ascent." This is of course at the foundation of the Christian myth, distended across the brief temporal cycle of crucifixion to ascension. What is so troubling to me about Actaeon is precisely the lack of "ascent." It seems to me the violence of that story amounts to a supervention, but it plays out horizontally, in a field that acknowledges its own mythic frame without transcending it. That's what's so shocking about it. It resists levitation.

Unfortunately I don't have *Earth Is Best* with me to review how Peter handles this notional ascent (I'm typing this from Newark Terminal C, which is no small player where gnostic horror is concerned). Is it possible to view *Phosphorescence* as a looking-out, *Earth Is Best* as a looking-down, and then *Hidden Eyes* as a looking-up?

Hidden Eyes interests me most as a map or mapping, a sort of star chart over or beneath which the psyche (some notional version of a psyche) is permitted to flow, perhaps similar to the superimposition of planes of polarized glass. And of course as a vehicle for discovery, self- or otherwise, just as Stephen says.

(As for allegory, I don't believe in it. We have a term for it, sure, but it's not real. Like the Tooth Fairy.)

[G.C. Waldrep]

Hi G.C. . . . on page 110 of *The Hidden Eyes of Things*, Peter lists the limits on his life (imposed by the stars). But in his frustrated naming of those limits, he drums up an exciting sense of God's grace. (Or so this was the experience that I had in my reading.) Peter concludes with his *discipline,* another quality imposed on him, but the only one that allows for independence. It's his ticket! I think of this discipline as obedience to God, rather than resisting what has been set for us (by God and the stars). The Jesuits say, "All is gift; all is grace." They really do mean *all* things. So, the astrology then struck me as Peter accepting his lot, wherein lies God's grace. Essentially, trust in God is the only way we get to maneuver freely while we're stuck here in material.

(Having said that, Peter might accidentally summon a demon, and he *knows* it.)

[Emily Tristan Jones]

———————————————————————————————

Dear All,

My active knowledge of English is ridiculously limited, which is why I choose not to talk (at least not too much), but I've been a fascinated and grateful reader of your comments on Peter's beautiful trilogy. What a special event! Please see below my visual note (appropriately taciturn, I hope) written a couple of years ago, dedicated to Peter, whose poetry recollects several traditions and fuses them with an acute sense of presence, of being here and now. "For *the language of God has no grammar; it consists only of names*" (quotation within quotation, within quotation), and then, just a few pages later:

"If you abolish the symbols, then you tear down the walls of your own house." They interact.

"Angel—for Peter O'Leary" goes with the following quotation from Nathaniel Mackey (and it is thanks to Peter again that I am familiar with Mackey's poetry):

". . . Day after day of
 the dead we were deaf, numb to
what the night before we said moved
                                         us,"

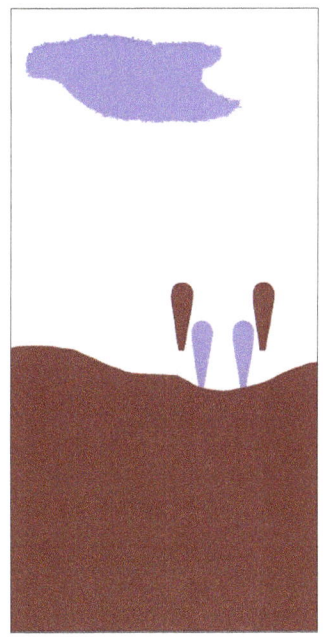

All the best to you all,

[Márton Koppány, Budapest, Hungary]

Dogs. His fucking dogs.

/some things thrown at the wall

'Tis. 'Tis. 'Ytis!
  Actæon . . .
  and a valley,
The valley is thick with leaves, with leaves, the trees,
The sunlight glitters, glitters a-top,
Like a fish-scale roof,
   Like the church roof in Poictiers
If it were gold.
   Beneath it, beneath it
Not a ray, not a slivver, not a spare disc of sunlight
Flaking the black, soft water;
Bathing the body of nymphs, of nymphs, and Diana,
Nymphs, white-gathered about her, and the air, air,
Shaking, air alight with the goddess
   fanning their hair in the dark,
Lifting, lifting and waffing:
Ivory dipping in silver,
   Shadow'd, o'ershadow'd
Ivory dipping in silver,
Not a splotch, not a lost shatter of sunlight.
Then Actæon: Vidal,
Vidal. It is old Vidal speaking,
   stumbling along in the wood,
Not a patch, not a lost shimmer of sunlight,
   the pale hair of the goddess.

The dogs leap on Actæon,
  "Hither, hither, Actæon,"
Spotted stag of the wood;
Gold, gold, a sheaf of hair,

104

Thick like a wheat swath,
Blaze, blaze in the sun,
     The dogs leap on Actæon.
Stumbling, stumbling along in the wood,
Muttering, muttering Ovid:
     "Pergusa . . . pool . . . pool . . . Gargaphia,
"Pool . . . pool of Salmacis."
 The empty armour shakes as the cygnet moves.
     (*Canto IV*)

Because I know Peter's read Norman O. Brown, I had the urge to just copy and paste the entirety of his [Brown's] chapter "Metamorphosis II: Actaeon" from *Apocalypse and / or Metamorphosis*, but it's too long (and not everything is pertinent), but a few clippings:

"Gargaphie and Golgotha are the same place: the place of skulls, and the mountain stained with the blood of beasts of every kind." Gargaphie = Golgotha = Calvary

"Human culture is human sacrifice, together with symbolic substitution: a ram, caught in a thicket by his horns, to take the place of Isaac. Symbolic substitution, or metamorphosis: turning the human victim into an animal totem: man into stag."

"Actaeon, the Holy Son of God, who took upon him the form of a servant, serf, cerf. And his own knew him not: the Jews, worse than dogs, did not recognize their master. The ghost of Actaeon appeared in a dream to his father Aristaeus, and begged him not to punish the dogs, saying Father, forgive them; for they knew not what they did." [He lists the sources for this excerpt, "Ovid, *Moralisé*, III, ll.624, 630. Philippians 2:7. Acts 13:27. Nonnus, *Dionysiaca*, V, ll.442, 445."]

He notes one variation of the story, from "Des Périers, *Cymbalum Mundi*, Dialogue IV," wherein "The dogs sated themselves in their own master's blood; Christ feeds his own with his own transubstantiated flesh. One version gives dogs the power of human speech; after they eat their master's tongue, the word made flesh."

Relation someone brought up of the "The Dogs" to the Bacchic scene:

"The dogs that know not their own master are mad dogs; the dogs of madness that tore Pentheus to pieces. Agave, his mother, knew not her own son. Lear's daughters knew not their own father. There is a vase painting of the stag man, attacked by his own bitches, with Lady Madness driving them on. Sweet heavens, do not make me mad." [Sources, Euripides, *Bacchae*, 977. Reinach, *Cultes* 3:24, fig. 5.]

He quotes the "Merciless Beauty" and Chaucer lingo lines from "Canto 81." which makes me think we cannot read this without looking back at Pound's version of Actaeon in "Canto 4" (and some other points where he comes up, as in "Canto 91"). Metamorphosis, theophany, which I think is pretty obviously what's happening here:

"But Cadmus's scion—Actaeon. There he is. His senses relaxing. Dilating." Dilation—"key" word for Emerson and Whitman—is a state vaguer but similar to Pound's *cogitatio, meditatio, contemplatio*, which are ascending steps with the aim the full communion with the divine (democracy, aristocracy; expanse flood, ascent). Actaeon is communing with the moon-goddess Diana. This pulls me over into

Frances Yates on Actaeon in her *The Occult Philosophy in the Elizabethan Age*. She's discussing Dürer's *Melencolia I* and *St Jerome in his Study*.

"Dürer's Melancholy is not in a state of depressed inactivity. She is in an intense visionary trance, a state guaranteed against demonic intervention by angelic guidance. She is not only inspired by Saturn as the powerful star-demon, but also by the angel of Saturn, a spirit with wings like the wings of Time.

"The starved dog is an important key to the meaning. This hound, in my opinion, is not yet another indication of a depressed mood of failure. It represents, I believe, the bodily senses, starved and under severe control in this first stage of inspiration, in which the inactivity is not representative of failure but of an intense inner vision. The Saturnian melancholic has 'taken leave of the senses' and is soaring in worlds beyond worlds in a state of visionary trance. The only sense which is alive and waking is the artist's hand, the hand of the *putto* recording the vision with his engraving tool—the hand of Dürer himself recording his psychology of inspiration in this marvelous engraving.

"The classic moralisation of the senses as hunting dogs is that given by Natalis Comes in his interpretation of the Actaeon fable, where Actaeon's dogs are the senses. The melancholy temperament was supposed to subdue the senses. A theorist on the humours defines Melancholy as 'the sweet sleep of the senses'. Or we may turn to John Milton who have in *Il Penseroso* the supreme poetic expression of the theory of inspired melancholy. 'Divinist Melancholy', whose black face hides a saintly visage [cf. Pound's "The Tree of Visages"

= "The Tree of Life" = (?) Peter's trees and leafage on page 17, "Diana's holy retreat"] too bright for human sense, is accompanied by 'spare diet', and in her soaring visions she escapes from the senses:

Or let my lamp at midnight hour
Be seen in some high lonely tower,
Where I may oft outwatch the Bear,
With thrice great Hermes, or unsphere
The spirit of Plato to unfold
What worlds or what vast regions hold
The Immortal mind *that hath forsook*
Her mansion in this fleshly nook;
And of those demons that are found
In fire, air, flood, or underground,
Whose power hath a true consent
With planet or with element.

"Milton's melancholy inspiration is also demonic, but a white ascetic magic (the starved dog of the senses), and connecting with higher realms of prophecy and angelic hierarchies. His Melancholy brings with her

Him that yon soars on golden wing,
Guiding the fiery wheeled throne
The Cherub Contemplation.

"Dürer's *Melencolia I* represented the first of Agrippa's series, the inspired artistic melancholy. There was also a stage relating to prophetic inspiration, and a stage in which the inspired intellect rose to the understanding of divine matters. All three are included in Milton's Melancholy, the saintly dark figure who seems to descend from Reuchlin via Agrippa. And all three may be intimated in Dürer's *Melencolia I* through the angelic wings which he gives to his black-faced figure."

Some of that relevant, some not. Brown again:

"Hunted by his own dogs, his companions, ravenous and riotous sycophants; a stag party, a wild hunt. Initiation is hazing: blind man's buff, with metamorphosis; bear baiting or stag baiting. Lucius turned into an ass, or Bottom in Midsummer Night's Dream. Sir John Falstaff in Merry Wives of Windsor, disguised as Herne the Hunter, with great ragged horns on his head. Falstaff: 'I do perceive that I am made an ass.' Falstaff's great ragged horns are his crown of thorns. The first step in the imitation of Christ: to be mocked. God is mocked. The stag is the hairy fool in the leather coat, much marked of the melancholy Jaques.

To day my Lord of Amiens and myself
Did steal behind him as he lay along
Under an oak, whose antique root peeps out
Upon the brook that brawls along this wood,
To the which place a poor sequestered stag,
That from the hunter's aim had ta'en a hurt,
Did come to languish; and indeed my lord,
The wretched animal heaved forth such groans
That their discharge did stretch his leathern coat
Almost to bursting, and the big round tears
Coursed one another down his innocent nose
In piteous chase; and thus the hairy fool,
Much marked of the melancholy Jaques,
Stood on th' extremest verge of the swift brook,

Augmenting it with tears.

"Lacrima Christi: a rich, sweet Neapolitan wine. [Sources: Shakespeare, *As You Like It*, act 2, scene l, ll. 29 43]' *on the extremest verge*: this is in Whitman's preface to *Leaves of Grass*: 'The greatest poet forms the consistence of what is to be from what has been and is. He drags the dead out of their coffins and stands them again on their feet . . .. he says to the past, Rise and walk before me that I may realize you. He learns the lesson . . .. he places himself where the future becomes present. The greatest poet does not only dazzle his rays over character and scenes and passions . . . he finally ascends and finishes all . . . he exhibits the pinnacles that no man can tell what they are for or what is beyond . . .. he glows a moment on the extremest verge. He is most wonderful in his last half-hidden smile or frown . . . by that flash of the moment of parting the one that sees it shall be encouraged or terrified afterward for many years."

"Actaeon submerged in animal. All verb. All summons. | Resonant aether." *Gyrus of his wild eyes. Law of death he registers. Its | gnostic instant.* Actaeon's "flash of the moment of parting." Theophany. Gyrus, circle, ring: gyre, cf Yeats. The gyre: I take this as penetrating sight, the 'senses relaxed', 'dilating', into the spiraling cosmos, eaten up and the coming-apart-of-all-things turning into "His mind's mad terminal dancing." *luminous rage* quenched.

"A summer rainstorm's incessant hiss and thunder." Brown again:

"The Wild Hunt, ghostly hunters who ride through the sky on stormy evenings, known in nearly all parts of the world.

. . . . [quoting *Henry IV, Part I*] 'Let us that are squires of the night's body be called thieves of the day's beauty; let us be 'Diana's foresters,' 'gentlemen of the shade' [cf. *Creased green with shade. . . . Green shade.* cp. Ronald Johnson's *green shadow run* when *the ends of the world shall turn*, a time when *worm shake the womb: I am poured out like water | into the dust of death.*], 'minions of the moon' . . . our noble and chaste mistress the moon, under whose countenance we steal.'"

Last thing: if you look at Pound's description of Diana, it's all radiating light, all on her head. I think one commentator says the head because she's taller than the others, the nymphs, there. Peter:

Like sunlight's silver-tipped spears. Like a new unanticipated
    thought.
Changing your life forever. She radiates. At him. Ever lasting.
    Eternity
involuntary taste. It shocks him. (*Earth Is Best*, 18)

Doesn't Peter use "compression and radiation" from Marie Curie (via Ronald Johnson) as epigraph to *Watchfulness*?
Pound:

Shadow'd, o'ershadow'd
Ivory dipping in silver,
Not a splotch, not a lost shatter of sunlight.

The light / shade in these lines (and in the whole encounter in both Pound's and Peter's paratranslations) has to be of interest given the "thick and dazzling darkness" which passage

Norman notes "Peter is utterly possessed by." "The shaman-poet must exhaust himself, bringing forth litanies . . . and give himself entirely to this worship. Whitman . . .. Because ecstasy is hard work, sacrificial labor of the greatest intensity." Billie: "the hard labor of ecstasy, the ordeal of initiation, the sacrifice vision demands": Dionysus as the patron saint of the visionary. His followers must lose their minds. And Acteon, torn apart (*Apart. Come.*) for the sake of a glimpse of God, for the sake of "a new unanticipated thought."

Good to look also at what the dogs do to light: "Dogs. Hexagons of sunlight they shatter in their mad dash. | Dogs. His fucking dogs." . . . And the LIST of the dogs, which Ovid, loving lists, provides to Peter, gives our poet the chance to go into litany mode, a kind of repetition again of a glory, but here of violent disrupters of light. ["And I'm back: daemonic Bromios. Disruptor of | earth's sacrament: life."] "Velocity's roar": I come across this sentence on 18 and think of Stephen Williams's "density and velocity." There is an ecstasy in naming, in listing these dogs' names; they are the names of the maenads who will rip apart Orpheus and leave his head floating down the Hebrus. Head with horns, an eclipse, Actaeon's name meaning (in one etymological path)—NOB again:

"Caught in a thicket by his horns: an eclipse; Actaeon, aktis, sun beam, eye beam. As the golden sun animal, the stag proceeds through the air spreading light which illuminates the mountain gorges. [A. Salmony, *Antler and Tongue*, 20.]"

From *Phosphorescence*:

With the oldest cherubim of knowledge,
the phanophagous cherubs, devouring

with their bodies the light they transform into scissoring flame
flared forth sword-like and brandished, unspeakably
world-like, fully
recklessly
Imagined. (4)

Dogs as phanophagous cherubs?

Phosphorescence: "The lying ladies. Practicing | false bloodless
rites: | communion with fame. Concerts with vanity" (55).
Earth Is Best: "Only his wounds | quench the Moon-goddess's
murderous luminous rage: rumor's | ambiguous violence" (19)
Fama rumor Dionysius the son of Semele, who is Cadmus's
daughter; Actaeon is "Cadmus's scion." The two are involved
in the same familial-mythological knot.

Okay, enough of this spew. Lot to stew on, and one could go
on and on like this.

[Steven Manuel]

Also, just that phrase, *Hexagons of ^sun^light*

Hexagons of sunlight they shatter in their mad dash.

HEXAGONS

I have the Kepes-edited *Module, Proportion, Symmetry, Rhythm*
in the VISION+VALUE SERIES (one of Ronald Johnson's
holy books, book-series). Flipping through at a medium pace I
came on things like Fuller's domes, structures of crystals, snail

forms, Bartok musical diagrams, etc. Hexagons popped up, this word/line coming back into mind.

[Steven Manuel]

---

the drama that becomes a feast by no means abstains from the originary dramatic of the ancient tragedy, on the contrary, the drama is led to its very essence. the feast fosters a consciousness that leads to the depths, to embracing our tragic reality. the world as a whole is to be accepted with all its extremes, its possibilities of happiness, of atrocities and the cruelty of death. failing, suffering, the tragic, the sacrifice, sado-masochistic cruelty can be viewed as a suddenly irruptive absurd hindering of the creative, in its essence the creative is bound to overcoming, repelling and removing hurdles. vivacious unfolding, ever-expanding effort in life, encounters natural hurdles and brings suffering and pain, spurs on to the pain-intermingled happiness of overcoming. the myth of death and resurrection presents itself as an allegory of the creative, the analytical technique of the play helps us to understand ourselves more totally, more uncompromisingly and more extensively, plumbing to the depths of the reality of our drives, usually remaining uncharted territory. repressed areas are unearthed and lived out. consciousness creeps and pushes to the grounds of energetics, the most sensitive moments of registering joyful lust are opened to consciousness. one essential impulse that determines humanity generally and drama specifically is taken into account. the need for abreaction is brought to consciousness and fulfilled. the drama brought to its essence is catharsis therapy, is comparable to psychoanalysis, only that the analytical process, in this case the dramatic process, is responsive to being exploited aesthetically. actions rising into a climax are deployed which trigger the very first elementary, intensive sensory sensations and lead later to an orgiastic, sado-masochist acting out by the participating performers and the audience. the associative impulse of classical psychoanalysis is replaced in the o.m. theatre by the sensory sensations evoked by the actions, which, once the censors are overcome, disinhibit and intoxicate, the actions with raw flesh, damp bowels still at body temperature, bloodied faeces, blood warmed from the slaughter, tepid water, etc provoke regressions towards anal sensuality. the joy at splashing around, spattering, pouring, smearing, soiling escalates into a joy in tearing raw flesh, a joy in trampling on the bowels. the dionysic dismemberment situation arises (the dismembered abreaction god dionysos enters the associative field). the dramatic rummages around in the joy in cruelty. chaos, an orgiastic intoxication, irrupts and breaks in over us. the intensity of the experience gives rise to a mystic of aggression and cruelty. the dramatic effect is grasped as the aesthetic intoxication of the audience and participants. hölderlin's understanding of the tragic is important here, when he sees that the power of nature and man's most inner core "limitlessly become one" in rage and that representing the tragic leads to transmitting "how god and man pair."

what's been dammed up for so long is released, the repressed becomes viewable, the endpoint of abreaction, the sado-masochist excess is reached, rendered aesthetically within the play the abreaction brings the cause of individual neuroses to consciousness. the collective-neurotic conditionality of sado-masochist myths of sacrifice is explicated.

with the conscious-raising rapturous frenzy of abreaction (the
endpoint of abreaction), the dramatic effect, having become
life, is brought to its climax, similar to the catastrophe of
the classical drama is reached, only that in the case of the
o.m. theatre the catastrophe is liberated from the tragic
hopelessness of the ancient drama by the neutralized aesthetic
bringing-to-awareness and rendering-viewable of the
repressed, through the far-reaching catharsis. the whole course
of life is condensed into a mythical experience. the rapturous
intensity of existence must spread over all areas of being,
across everyday life. a world overcome with cheerful joviality
should allow us to serenely immerse in all possibilities of
enjoyment. all the senses have to be intensified and sensitized.
the extreme sublimation of the excessive is the upsurge of
the intensely felt liveliness spreading through us, rising to
the joyous rapture of the state of altruistic love. love not
understood as commandment but as state, as the highest state
of existence, as a state of being. love is the mystic of being
spread across the whole of life.
Hermann Nitsch

Ataxia - Aids is Fun / Derek Jarman

[See: 氷の炎]

(You may want to lower your volume before you click that)

[Devin King]

Emily, I agree with you. Pete doesn't deserve excommunication for dabbling in astrology, but rather for his adoration of Gnostic archons. :)

Márton, I wish I could communicate as well as you.

[Michael O'Leary]

I wish I could see you and Peter again, Michael. That's for sure. :-)
All best to you (and to the whole "group"),

[Márton Koppány]

Márton, your *Angel* could be an emblem for the whole trilogy.

Astrology as a system for knowing, mapping, yes. Insight more than divination.

What if the zodiac represents not an outer limit, a band
beyond which the Empyrean blazes in all its glory
but a reflective limit
the ecliptical mirror
redirecting the spiritual gaze
inward
to its volatile core
of potable gold?

(*Hidden Eyes*, 6)

The poet/persona of *Hidden Eyes* only says "I" a half dozen times in the whole book—he's made known mostly by the "astrologer" who creates a lyric "I" from a lyric "you" in an extended catechism, at once a ciphering and a deciphering of self, and of *being* itself—and a reckoning, which gives the book its feel of the liminal, a threshold. Who am I? What can be known now, said now?

If the poet has summoned demons, it's a bringing forth from within. The Gospel of Thomas says that will save him. Is that heresy? The trilogy is itself a gnostic gospel, no? "What if the god is a mushroom after all? / And resurrection is a spoor." (*Earth Is Best*, 73) Have all the new testaments been written? If so, what are we doing here?

The updated Milton and Yeats at the beginning and end, are two of the strangest poems in *Hidden Eyes,* and I wonder what others make of them. The unfathomable Blakean "the joy of heaven is continual battle," the "harm" in "harmony," and the "dragon of flame whose secret lawgiver is the holy spirit." Here, Yes and No (in all their manifestations) constantly resurrect each other—the creative movement of Mind, both lyric and cosmic. This cannot be fixed.

"The Jesuits say, 'All is gift; all is grace.' They really do mean *all* things," as you say, Emily.

"the extreme sublimation of the excessive is the upsurge of the intensely felt liveliness spreading through us, rising to the joyous rapture of the state of altruistic love. love not understood as commandment but as state, as the highest state of existence, as a state of being. love is the mystic of being spread across the whole of life." *Hermann Nitsch, via Devin, Ox*

I'm drawn to the *mystic state of being* given voice in the poetry of this trilogy, its rapture and reverence. In *How to Know Higher Worlds,* Rudolf Steiner says there is no spiritual progress without reverence—reverence comes first.

fully/recklessly/imagined, the poetry of *Hidden Eyes* is sometimes shockingly beautiful.
From the Venus section:

> . . . That day you

took the dew squeezed through a gauze of woven fibers and
    drew it up
into an eyedropper, depositing it in an apothecary's
vial. The past you expressed
you rolled into straws you
dried in the light of
the daystar.
        Catching fire, the straws
fumed in a censer, a beautiful thing, an offering fit
for Love's prime tastes.
          And then you summoned her, mistress
of good and gall, and she frightened you and
showed you her raptures, and wiving you she stroked
your needs and
holds you still
in her
thrall. (50)

Peter relates this story about a conversation he had with Joe Donahue:

Some years ago, after Karen King's book *What Is Gnosticism?* was published, Joe and I were talking about it and while agreeing to its obvious excellence, he expressed frustration that it effectively debunked the idea of the existence of a band of mystic-minded Christian heretical psychonauts (in so many words), at least as a unified group of any sort. Joe said of the Gnostic mythos, "It's so beautiful, it must be true."

[Billie Chernicoff]

"It's so beautiful, it must be true!" . . . but some beautiful things are forbidden by other beautiful things.

[Emily Tristan Jones]

There is a detachment acquired by intellectuals that makes the occult permissible for them alone, isn't there? Michael, that's my beef with the gnostic stuff, and with the stars. I can read someone's diary to find exciting truths, but I shouldn't be reading it. I'm not excused just for being able to read it very well. Yes, *of course* astrology provides insight, mapping, a way of knowing (G.C.). It's beautiful. But is it not real? I want poetry to be real! And I think that Peter's poetry is about as real as it gets. (Important to note: Peter's Church doesn't say that divination doesn't work. It just says don't do it.)

[Emily Tristan Jones]

Just now able to return to our conversation, & very glad for it. Steven's wonderful working through of multiple Actaeon's I'll need to return to often. But even in a glancing read, can feel an aspect of Peter's larger mythological approach, per *Earth Is Best*, of a given mythic type or persona as a kind of mycological irruption, as if myth itself is one of the ways in which a dead rote humanity is returned to a living possibility of one.

Started rereading *Hidden Eyes* yesterday, feeling the utter surety of the lyric line as a full arrival into the poetic powers Peter has been seeking. I think it's a wondrous book. & so a scattering of thoughts, to add some loam to the community garden—

*

Still reveling in the lucky coincidence of our 40 day sojourn with the trilogy and reading Sewell's *The Orphic Voice* at the same time. "PO'L" has become a common marginalia in the book, & I thought I might just offer a few passages:

> (Quoting Goethe) "The central point and very basis of his existence was poetry as a kind of life-force, increasingly active and developing inwardly and outwardly."

I keep finding in the trilogy evidence of or experiment in Emerson's sense of reciprocity as the most fundamental universal law. The inward and the outward are simultaneous events, and a development in one is so in the other.

To see the whole of nature as a generative process is part of postlogic, and allows the thinking organism to figure in itself the process it is reflecting upon.

The order one finds in the world—the within the mind of *Phosphorescence*, the within the earth of *Earth Is Best*, the *ouranos* of *Hidden Eyes*—creates parallel order in the self. Self and cosmos as same stuff, beholden to same laws: ". . . a mythological vision of the relationship between man's mind and the natural universe." I can begin to imagine the Trilogy as Wordsworth's *Prelude* turned inside-out.

*

& Parmenides, mentioned last by Michael I think, feels bedrock strata here. Peter might well be becoming our primary poet of the copulative infinitive: *to is*.

[Dan Beachy-Quick]

Cartography—the figure of the map—is, I think, a really useful way to think about *Hidden Eyes*. I'm glad G.C. noted that above (and I have to agree, Liz Gray's *Salient* is another exemplary work of cartography). A map is a projection. As Peter says in the afterwood to *Hidden Eyes*, "Astrology avails the experience and metaphoric power of projection." Here I take *projection* to mean *imagination*. Now I don't believe in astrology any more than G.C. believes in allegory, but as far as I'm concerned, whether astrology is true or not is simply beside the point. The truth of *Hidden Eyes*—its force—lies in the affinities the book finds between the mind of the poet and where the planets sat at the moment of his birth. It's an audaciously Dantean project.

Early in Philip Pullman's novel, *The Secret Commonwealth*, Sebastian Makepeace—an alchemist, no less—says, "You won't understand anything about the imagination until you realize that it's not about making things up, it's about perception." The planetary map of the unconscious in *Hidden Eyes* is the product of a deeply perceptive imagination.

[John Tipton]

Those aspects that resisted interpretation were considered *decorative*, while those too charged with meaning were labeled *ornamental*.
Roberto Calasso, *Tiepolo Pink*

The void was too full of meaning
so it ornamented itself
with the world.

The dark was too full of meaning
so it ornamented itself
with light.

Fate was too full of meaning
so it ornamented itself
with chance.

History was too full of meaning
so it ornamented itself
with apocalypse.

God was too full of meaning
so he ornamented himself
with humankind.

And humankind, cracked cup,
can never fill with meaning.
They live and die instead.

[Stephen Williams]

---

less a work of the mind than of affects
brought forth form the inner nature
here sung in these odes
Urbanity in externals, virtu in internals

...

periplum, not as land looks on a map
but as sea bord seen by men sailing
Now tarters in the murk night
sent great numbers of sojers with lanthorns
which they held up very high
          and thus spread light on proceedings

Canto LIX

Paul Klee, *Ad Marginem*

[Devin King]

AT THE GATES OF DELIRIUM

Again, mostly for [Devin, Ox] [See: Yes, "The Gates of Delirium"]

Since we've drifted into *Hidden Eyes* I've been asking myself along with Emily and G.C. why astrology, exactly? What does it do that you can't get from, say, scapulimancy, ouija, Rorschach tests, or Tarot? Despite his gnostic antics, I don't think Pete is actually interested in messing with demons. So ouija is out. And that territory has been well covered. But Rorschach is getting closer. Tarot too. They have an element of the parlor game, table talk, bullshitting, and having fun. I've listened to my kids and nephews and niece and their friends talk for hundreds of hours, asking, "what am I like?" Unlike Tarot, which could also be considered a mapping to objectify one's interiority, astrology includes an effective or algorithmic procedure as part of the pattern recognition, something Pete emphasizes in the afterword: "magnificent and minute clockwork dialing the heavens into finer attunements depending on how subtly you wish to adjust it" (180). It's not just schema; Pete loves process too. And process allows him to imagine apocalypse, something that looms over the trilogy, especially in the form of environmental collapse. In that sense, I see astrology and Tarot as subsets of Monte Carlo methods, where a state space is described and combined in an algorithmic procedure less about a mastery of time and more an attempt to manage expectations by minimizing surprise. The astrological states here are archetypal and the procedure is combinatorial, but the interpretation represents a commitment.

Stephen Williams, I mentioned earlier something about the one-way action of the mapping in *Hidden Eyes*, but that was wrong. I was still under the spell of the Mars section, which, as Norman rightly pointed out in the Zoom reading, is among the most objective sections of the poem. By contrast, "At the Gates of Delirium" uses the schema to retrospectively reinterpret his experience as a disciple of Ronald Johnson, cultivating the "studied rebellion" of esotericism. But he still ends up recognizing that, rather than being a sage, he just has a lot of anxiety and tries to get by with a little help from his friends.

For a long time, I felt that Pete's most original contribution to poetry was the reclamation of anxiety as a religious experience, that these psychic phenomena can't be solved by root cause analysis, but rather endured, ingested, and incorporated like grace itself. Yes, Pete loves Freud, but as the last great figure of the Enlightenment, it's an odd choice. I've even wondered whether he wasn't, by reading Freud so closely, just trying to keep his enemies close. Through Teilhard de Chardin, he reclaims evolution as a religious experience too. Not that he's advocating a kind of intelligent design—what's not intelligent about natural selection anyway? But there is something anti-enlightenment about Pete's esotericism, an attempt to join the macrocosm to the microcosm through astrology and mushrooms, to argue that this emergence of consciousness is a reunion with the divine mind, that things are interrelated without necessary causal relations.

So what are the fruits? Despite his apparent heterodox esoteric syncretism, it's all to bring to the work

                                        . . . gold and silver and
dearworth gemstones
and the hair of a goat
just as God bid

I can think of little poetry as joyful, reverent, and devoted.

[Michael O'Leary]

P.S. DBQ, have you read Márton Koppány's "To Be or To
Be"? Pure Parmenidean power.

Three unevenly distributed questions intersect in this
discussion of the trilogy: where does this come from (a
question of origins); what do I believe (the question of faith);
and how do I express this (the question of language).

There's no focal origin mythos, no vision of Ezekiel in a tree
when I was five, rather the prolonged miseries of an alcoholic
household and the comforts of books and music (mostly
science fiction and fantasy, prog, heavy metal, and indie rock),
and a truly heroic consumption of television and Mountain
Dew. Poetry didn't come until college. Yeats, Rilke, Duncan,
Whitman, in that order.

As a Catholic, I participate actively in the sacraments—I
receive the Eucharist, I go to confession, I have a daily
contemplative prayer practice (it involves the Jesus prayer);
I'm a catechist (seventh grade); I'm a lector; I do a lot of
spiritual writing for my parish (reflections on scripture),

which includes co-authoring three workbooks for lectors and proclaimers of the Word, all of which I find immensely fulfilling. Theologically, I'm inclined toward mysticism; practically, I'm drawn to magic, what Yeats calls "the darker powers." I don't experience any of this as a contradiction but rather as an intuitive and obvious co-inherence. In the Magi is the archetype for a life in faith.

I've always been more interested in questions of how—transmission and transmutation—than in questions of why—origins and being. Jung rather than Plato. Theophany (and angelophany) rather than the existence of God. Poetry manifests vision in language. The transmission of that vision and its subsequent transmutations absorb my imagination utterly. Revelation. Apocalypse. The Visionary Recital—what Dante calls "the high things." My understanding of allegory is Dante's—which Eliot glosses as *clear visual images*. To see things clearly is to enter the realm of allegory. The higher realm—the realm of anagogy—you ascend to by the uplift of interpretation, insight, lightning strike.

In the summer of 2018, I was invited to a symposium on Christian poetics at Calvin College in Grand Rapids, Michigan (G.C. was there as well), for which I was asked to produce a statement. Modeled directly on an essay by Pierre Teilhard de Chardin, whose title I borrowed, "How I Believe" is as complete a statement as I've made about what I imagine I'm doing. Because it remains unpublished and because it speaks directly to this merry and beloved company, I offer it here with an expression of deep and anagogically inflected thanks.

[Peter O'Leary, Oak Park, Illinois]

+++

How I Believe

after Pierre Teilhard de Chardin

I. I believe in the earth, source of all greatness and power.
II. I believe the imagination reflects divine consciousness.
III. I believe in magic; specifically, in the sacro-magical sciences.
IV. I believe the apocalypse unbinds love and changes all things.

Prologue

The greatest poetry is Earth-borne in its language, imaginal in its psychism, magical in its incantation, and apocalyptic in its vision. Whitman:

> I find I incorporate gneiss and coal and long-
>   threaded moss and fruits and grains and esculent
>   roots,
> And am stucco'd with quadrupeds and birds all over
>   . . . (40)

A poetry of transformation and incarnation, of emanation and ebullition.

I. I believe in the earth, source of all greatness and power.

Earth Is Best. The Earth is our science, its core and circumference, all that we know coming from and going into the Earth. Father Pierre Teilhard de Chardin, writing in China in 1934 a theology of evolution (but barred by his vow of obedience from publishing it—this wouldn't happen until after his death in 1955 when his vow was concluded), speculates:

> If, as the result of some interior revolution, I were to lose in succession my faith in Christ, my faith in a personal God, and my faith in spirit, I feel that I should continue *to believe* invincibly *in the world.* The world (its value, its infallibility and its goodness)—that, when all is said and done, is the first, the last, and the only thing in which I believe. It is by faith that I live. And it is to this faith, I feel, that at the moment of death, rising above all doubts, I shall surrender myself. (99)

Natural powers shape our lives. Living forms absorb our imaginations. Chthonos as cosmos. In 1856, Whitman wrote a "Poem of the Sayers of the Words of the Earth," which begins:

> Earth, round, rolling, compact—suns, moons, animals—all these words,
> watery, vegetable, sauroid advances—beings, premonitions, lispings of the future—these arevast words.(160)

Birdsong, springtime, sunlight, the Newtonian orbital lock of the Moon, its drift across the unwinking eye of the Sun in a total solar eclipse: these and thousands of other things join me in my life to the Earth in which like Teilhard I believe utterly.

> I swear there is no greatness or power that does not
> emulate those of the earth!
> I swear there can be no theory of any account,
> unless it corroborate the theory of the earth!
> No politics, art, religion, behaviour, or what not, is
> of account, unless it compare with the amplitude
> of the earth,
> Unless it face the exactness, vitality, impartiality,
> rectitude of the earth. (164)

By Whitman's reckoning, expressions of greatness emulate the Earth itself. Does our consciousness emulate the Earth? It does. In that the Earth, as stated, is our science, the core and circumference of what we know, it does. William James compared it to a river or a stream. He calls it "at every stage a theatre of simultaneous possibilities." It's the entirety of our feeling for life and, like the Earth itself, it is evolving and changing. James asserts:

> We may, if we like, by our reasonings unwind things
> back to that black and jointless continuity of space
> and moving clouds of swarming atoms which science
> calls the only real world. But all the while the world
> *we* feel and live in will be that which our ancestors
> and we, by slowly cumulative strokes of choice,
> have extricated out of this, like sculptors, by simply
> rejecting certain portions of the given stuff (288-9).

Teilhard describes this process of the development of consciousness as "co-reflection," an act of increasingly complex interiorization in which our awareness intensifies our presence, our thought and feeling thickening or "centrating" our place in creation. "We now see beings as like threadless fibres, woven into a universal process." (104)

And yet, because of our consciousness, we present to ourselves "a monstrous stumbling block." "It is a curious thing," writes Teilhard, "[M]an, the centre and creator of all science, is the only object which our science has not yet succeeded in including in a homogeneous representation of the universe." (105) Put another way, we are using consciousness to understand consciousness and its evolution. The stumbling block, then, is our enormous arrogance blithely permitted by shortsightedness. This is where sin comes from. "The only thing that God demands from us, mortals," advises Saint Symeon the New Theologian, "is that we do not sin." In meeting this demand, we fail constantly. Paul refers to sin as *hamartia* (I Cor. 6:18), the fatal somatic flaw, embodied. If this problem has a solution, the imagination shows the way.

II. I believe the imagination reflects divine consciousness.

And the imagination is vision. "The soul never thinks without an image," wrote Aristotle. (225) We live in a time of spiritual blindness. It's immoral. A spiritually sightless immorality pushes us to blunder through life. And our souls grow more faint.

The soul is nourished by images and the greatest image is that of God, who is total vision, image heaped upon image. In the Catholic Church, crucial emphasis is placed on grace, on receiving it. Grace defines your spiritual life. In the Orthodox churches, the emphasis falls on mystical union with God, or *theosis*. I prefer this emphasis—there is the continual forgiveness of sins (without which friendship cannot exist, according to Blake) but also the sense of striving through sin, through the fatal somatic flaw, to God. "Union with God is a mystery which is worked out in human persons," writes Vladimir Lossky in *The Mystical Theology of the Orthodox Church* (217). This union is a vision of transfigured light: "Those who have not seen this light, have not seen God: for God is Light" (218). God is not foreign to our experience, the primary visional expression of which is light.

> How is it we have walkd thro fires & yet are not consumd
> How is it that all things are changd even as in ancient
>   times (475)

All things are changed in the soul nourished on the image of God as transfigured light magnifying imagination, which starts as words and transforms into total vision.

A Monk of the Eastern Church explains that while divine locutions and visions may coincide, the gift of insight belongs to a higher level:

> We could therefore define every vision granted to us on earth as an anticipation and reflection, however dim, of the vision of God in heaven. Generally speaking, there is an ascending gradation in the external phenomena of the spiritual life. This gradation begins with "words" and finishes with "vision." At first one listens to God, at the end one sees Him. (100)

In the imagination, the world is incarnated, becoming God. In her poem, "In the Spirit There Are No Accidents," Fanny Howe writes:

> God is already ahead and waiting: the future is full.
> One steps timidly over the world;
> the other is incomparable.
> The house is there. The door is there . . . others . . .
> But for you they make no sound when you're so far.
> I know the bench is by the pond tomorrow
> when I can follow the streets to it by heart.
> Yes, streets. Yes, heart.
> Nightwalk of faith, chromosomes live in the past.
> The land is an incarnation
> like a hand on a hand on an arm asking *do you know me?*
>
> (115)

The question to which Meister Eckhart provides seven centuries before Howe wrote her poem an answer: "God 'becomes' God when all creatures speak God forth: there 'God' is born. When I was still in the ground, in the depths, in the flood and source of the Godhead, no one asked me where I wished to go or what I was doing. But as I flowed forth, all creatures uttered: 'God'" (234).

Divinization is utterly creaturely. It happens through the senses, vision especially, but all of which harmonize in the imagination. One of the great visionary harmonizations in the Christian imagination is the Celestial Hierarchy described by Dionysius in a work of the same name, consisting of revolving holy orders of angels mounting through an intermediating mesocosm from the visible into the invisible, from angels, archangels, and principalities (the third—lowest—triad), through authorities, powers, and dominions (the second triad), to the thrones, cherubim, and seraphim (the first triad). The highest triad is also the intensest, in actuality closest to God. In Canto XXVIII of the *Paradiso*, Dante is granted a glimpse of the whole hierarchy's ebullient, circumcinct operation. Clarifying the motion of the first triad, Beatrice says to Dante the Pilgrim, "Thus rapidly [the Seraphim and Cherubim] follow their own bands, / To be as like the point as most they can, / And can as far as they are high in vision" (Lines 100-2, translated by Henry Wadsworth Longfellow). How are they as far as they are high in vision? How does that work? Upward they gaze but downward they prevail—like light in a gravity well. Beatrice explains:

> And thou shouldst know that they all have delight
>   As much as their own vision penetrates
>   The Truth, in which all intellect finds rest.
> From this it may be seen how blessedness
>   Is founded on the faculty which sees,
>   And not in that which loves, and follows next. (Lines 106-11)

(Following Saint Thomas Aquinas, Dante believed that the intellect, which sees, and not the will, which loves, enables blessedness.) Putting things more succinctly perhaps, Blake, in the second book of *Milton*, insists, "The Imagination is not a State: it is the Human Existence itself" (586).

III. I believe in magic; specifically, in the sacro-magical sciences.

The signature of all things is a doctrine of hiddenness and revelation. The ancestor for the word *magic* is the Greek phrase *magike techne*, magic art, attested in the Septuagint. Historian of religion Lawrence Sullivan writes, "From the point of view of many magicians, magic aims to close the gap between a sign and the real power to which it refers. Magical speech and acts bring into the light of day the power and truth that lie hidden behind the signs of ordinary discourse and gesture. Hidden realities are made visible in the fantastic images of the magician" (xi). The scholar of esotericism Antoine Faivre refers to this exchange from hidden to revealed sign, from microcosm to macrocosm, as the "homo-analogical principle" or "doctrine of correspondences," which says, "things that are similar exert an influence on one another by virtue of the correspondences that unite all visible things to one another and to invisible realities as well" (3).

Alchemists spoke of their work as a *magnum opus*, an ongoing work of the creation in which they harmonized, through an arduous but metamorphic process, their interior realities with the larger cosmic reality. Describing this process, Carl Jung wrote, "For the alchemists the process of individuation represented by the *opus* was an analogy of the creation of the world, and the *opus* itself an analogy of God's work of creation. Man was seen as a microcosm, a complete equivalent of the world as miniature" (para. 550). This work is essentially daemonic—putting the alchemist or magician through his involvement with interiority in direct contact with fate, with the stirrings of power. In *The H.D. Book*, Robert Duncan professes this conviction clearly, when he writes:

> The work itself is the transformation of the ground. In this ground the soul and the world are one in a third hidden thing, in imagination of which the work arises. It is the work of creation then. It is Poetry, a Making. It is also the *opus alchymicum* of Hermetic and

Rosicrucian alchemy. The rhymes of this poetry are correspondences, workings and figures and patterns in which we apprehend the whole we do not see. (79)

To write a poem is an essentially magical act, to move from nothing (chaos) to something (cosmos), advancing in increments the work of creation, flashing it forth in a divine vision. Poetry is one of the sacro-magical sciences, perhaps the most primordial of them all. It is, to use a phrase I coined in a poem, an esotericism of the actual, something hidden and true in plain sight. And this act of revealing the hidden, showing it forth in the poem, is an act of transformation, of transubstantiation, of communion. H.D., writing in *Tribute to the Angels*, the second part of her magnificent *Trilogy*, proclaims of this new sensation, this ritual vision that is happening everywhere out of the ruins of the great catastrophic bombings of London in May 1944:

> We are part of it;
> we admit the transubstantiation,
>
> not God merely in bread
> but God in the other-half of the tree
>
> that looked dead—
> did I bow my head?
>
> did I weep? my eyes saw,
> it was not a dream
>
> yet it was a vision,
> it was a sign,

it was *the Angel which redeemed me,*
it was the Holy Ghost—

a half-burnt-out apple-tree
blossoming;

this is the flowering of the rood,
this is the flowering of the wood

where Anneal, we pause and give
thanks that we rise again from death and live. (87)

Hiddenness, revelation, daemonism, transformation, communion, resurrection, thanksgiving: these are the terms of a magical Christian poetics.

IV. I believe the apocalypse unbinds love and changes all things.

And apocalypse. Perhaps, of these terms, apocalypse above all. Apocalypse, in terms of scripture, is both genre and form. The genre is fantastical, phantasmatic. The form is visionary, often in the first person. It's the closest literary expression to a dream. The apocalyptic worldview demonstrates what Joseph Dan, the scholar of Jewish mysticism, says of the Kabbalistic worldview of the Zohar, that "everything is a reflection of everything else" (33). The Book of Revelation is as poetically provocative as it is confusing and obscure. Its vision is thearchical, cosmologically terminal, imaginal, draconian, and distortive. It has been many a fool's urgent temple and prognostic laughingstock. It presents the richest and most compelling symbolic reality in Christendom. I have been to the island of Patmos, and have climbed to the Grotto of the

Apocalypse, entering the cave where Saint John saw those colossal visions (and where, according to legend, Prohoros, his amanuensis, recorded them for him), and I have looked to the ceiling of the cave cleft by a triune suture—the lightning of the apocalypse having split it thus—and I have lain my head in the divot in the cave's wall where Saint John lay to receive the visions, and I have felt there the sutures of my skull loosening in a tremoring tripartite shudder and I knew it all to be true.

In Revelation is found the single-most important command to poets: *What thou seest, write in a book*. In this way (as H.D. affirms in *Trilogy*), poets witness the making of all things new.

Teilhard de Chardin picks up the story: "Under the influence of [segregation and aggregation], which is almost entirely hidden, the universe is being transformed and is maturing all around us . . . One day," he writes:

> the Gospel tells us, the tension gradually accumulating between humanity and God will touch the limits prescribed by the possibilities of the world. And then will come the end. Then the presence of Christ, which has been silently accruing in things, will suddenly be revealed—like a flash of light from pole to pole. Breaking through all the barriers within which the veil of matter and the water-tightness of souls have seemingly kept it confined, it will invade the face of the earth. And, under the finally liberated action of the true affinities of being, the spiritual atoms of the world will be borne along by a force generated by the powers of cohesion proper to the universe itself and will occupy, whether within Christ or without Christ (but always under the influence of Christ), the

place of happiness or pain designated for them by the
living structure of the Pleroma . . . Like lightning, like
a conflagration, like a flood, the attraction exerted
by the Son of Man will lay hold of all the whirling
elements in the universe so as to reunite them or
subject them to His body. (133-4)

This is entirely, utterly an act of imagination, things seen
whose force urges us to awaken and to come away, love
unbound by any strictures, a flame joined in a sheet of flame
to the consummation of creation. Once again, Blake:

> The Imagination is not a State: it is the Human Existence
>   itself
> Affection or Love becomes a State, when divided from
>   Imagination
> The Memory is a State always, & the Reason is a State
> Created to be Annihilated & a new Ratio Created
> Whatever can be Created can be Annihilated Forms
>   cannot
> The Oak is cut down by the Ax, the Lamb falls by the
>   knife
> But the Forms Eternal Exist, For-ever. Amen
>   Hallelujah (586)

Finally, like Christ, *the Earth can clasp me in her giant arms.*
How can the words of my poem bear up the Earth with
greater strength? How can vision in my poem be more acute,
more divine in attunement? How can my poem be more
magical? How can my poem unbind love and begin to change
all things? And what are the things that are left to see and say?

BIBLIOGRAPHY

Absu. *Barathrum: V.I.T.R.I.O.L.* Gothic / Osmose, 1993. "The advisory circle – Learning owl reappears." *YouTube,* uploaded by voolante. 6 October 2011. https://youtu. be/2k3RJrPlM38.

Alighieri, Dante. *The Divine Comedy.* Translated by C.H. Sisson. Oxford: Oxford University Press, 1992.

—. **Vita Nuova.** Translation by Mark Musa. Oxford: Oxford University Press, 1992.

The Bible: Authorized King James Version with Apocrypha. Oxford: Oxford University Press, 1997.

Brodsky, Joseph. *Less Than One: Selected Essays.* New York: Farrar, Straus and Giroux, 1986.

Brown, Norman O. *Apocalypse and / or Metamorphosis.* Berkeley, CA: University of California Press, 1991.

Calasso, Roberto. *Tiepolo Pink.* New York: Alfred A. Knopf, 2009.

Catechism of the Catholic Church: The CTS Definitive and Complete Edition. London: Catholic Truth Society, 2016.

"A Conversation Between Peter O'Leary and David Bentley Hart." *YouTube,* uploaded by Leaves in the Wind. 15 March 2023. https://youtu.be/NyJczIlZ2B0.

Cook, Francis H. *Hua-yen Buddhism: The Jewel Net of Indra.* University Park and London: The Pennsylvania State University Press, 1977.

"Covenant of the pieces." *Wikipedia,* Wikimedia Foundation. 11 April 2023. https://en.wikipedia.org/wiki/Covenant_of_ the_pieces - :~:text=Covenants in biblical times were,literally as "to cut".

Dickinson, Emily. *Selected Letters.* Edited by Thomas H. Johnson. Cambridge, MA: Harvard University Press, 1986.

—. **"Spit the Lark—and you'll find the Music (861)."** *Genius.com*, ML Genius Holdings LLC. Accessed 15 June 2023.

Duncan, Robert. *The Collected Later Poems and Plays.* Edited by Peter Quartermain. Berkeley, CA: University of California Press, 2014.

—. **The H.D. Book.** Edited by Michael Boughn and Victor Coleman. Berkeley, CA: University of California Press, 2011.

Eliot, T.S. *Collected Poems: 1909-1962.* London: Faber & Faber, 2002.

Emerson, Lake & Palmer. *Welcome Back My Friends to the Show That Never Ends – Ladies and Gentlemen.* Manticore, 1974.

Euripides. *Bacchae. The Greek Plays: Sixteen Plays by Aeschylus, Sophocles, and Euripides.* Translated by Emily Wilson. Edited by Mary Lefkowitz and James Romm. New York: Modern Library, 2016.

The Gospel of Thomas: The Hidden Sayings of Jesus. Translated by Marvin Meyer. Interpretation by Harold Bloom. San Francisco, CA: HarperCollins, 1992.

Harper, Douglas. "Etymology of apodictic." *Online Etymological Dictionary,* https://www.etymonline.com/word/apodictic. Accessed 15 June 2023.

—. **"Etymology of experiment."** *Online Etymology Dictionary,* https://www.etymonline.com/word/experiment. Accessed 15 June, 2023.

Hart, David Bentley. "The Anti-Theology of the Body." *The New Atlantis,* https://www.thenewatlantis.com/publications/the-anti-theology-of-the-body. Accessed 31 August, 2024.

Heraclitus. *The Cosmic Fragments: A Critical Study.* Edited and translated by G.S. Kirk. Cambridge: Cambridge University Press, 1954.

Finkelstein, Norman. Book Review of *The Hidden Eyes of Things,* by Peter O'Leary. *Restless Messengers: Poetry in Review.* https://www.poetryinreview.com/reviews/hidden_eyes_of_things.html. Accessed 15 June 2023.

Fletcher, Angus. *Allegory: The Theory of a Symbolic Mode.* Princeton, NJ: Princeton University Press, 2012.

Frye, Northrop. *Fearful Symmetry: A Study of William Blake.* Edited by Nicholas Halmi. Toronto: University of Toronto Press, 2004.

—. ***The Great Code: The Bible and Literature.*** Edited by Alvin A. Lee. Toronto: University of Toronto Press, 2006.

Fulton, Hamish. *Small Birds / A Continuous 101 Mile Walk without sleep / Country Roads Kent and Sussex England / Full Moon 10 11 November 1992 (from the portfolio Dear Dear Stieglitz).* 1994. Gelatin silver print on baryta paper. Scottish National Gallery of Modern Art (Modern One).

"The Gates of Delirium by Yes in 1080p HD HQ." *YouTube,* uploaded by vzqk50HD. 18 November 2012. https://youtu.be/EdmUAsU2eXI.

Gray, Jr., Elizabeth T. *Salient.* New York: New Directions, 2020.

Harrison, Jane Ellen. *Prolegomena for the Study of Greek Religion.* Princeton, NJ: Princeton University Press, 1991.

Hill, Geoffrey. *Broken Hierarchies: Poems 1952-2012.* Edited by Kenneth Haynes. Oxford: Oxford University Press, 2013. Izmirlieva, Valentina. *All the Names of the Lord: Lists, Mysticism, and Magic.* Chicago, IL: University of Chicago Press, 2008.

Jarman, Derek. *Ataxia – Aids is Fun*. 1993. Oil paint on canvas. Tate Britain.

Johnson, Ronald. *ARK*. Chicago, IL: Flood Editions, 2013.

Johnson, Samuel. *The Lives of the Most Eminent English Poets; With Critical Observations on Their Works, Volume I*. Edited by Roger Lonsdale. Oxford/New York: Oxford University Press, 2006.

Jones, David. *Epoch and Artist*. London: Faber & Faber, 1959.

Julian of Norwich. *Revelations of Divine Love*. Translation by

Barry Windeatt. Oxford: Oxford University Press, 2015.

Klee, Paul. *Ad Marginem*. 1930 / 1935-1936. Wasserfarbe und Feder auf Lackgrundierung auf Karton auf Keilrahmen genagelt, rückseitig weisse Grundierung mit Farbspuren; Keilrahmen mit Gaze überzogen. Kuntsmuseum Basel.

Kepes, Gyorgy, editor. *VISION + VALUE SERIES: Module, Proportion, Symmetry, Rhythm*. New New York: George Braziller, Inc., 1966.

"Kerygma." *Wikipedia*, Wikimedia Foundation. 22 February 2022. https://en.wikipedia.org/wiki/Kerygma.

Koppány, Márton. "Angel–for Peter O'Leary."

"氷の炎." *YouTube*, uploaded by Les Rallizes Dénudés（裸のラリーズ）. 14 February 2023. https://youtu.be/Tg8Yj_hA6qQ.

Liddell, Henry George and Robert Scott. "κήρυγμα" and "κηρύσσω". *A Greek-English Lexicon, with a Revised Supplement*. Revised and augmented by Henry Stuart Jones, with the assistance of Roderick McKenzie. Supplement edited by P.G.W. Glare, with the assistance of A.A. Thompson. Ninth Revised Edition. Oxford: Oxford University Press, 1996.

Luther, Martin. "The Heidelberg Disputation." *The Ninety-Five Theses and Other Writings.* Edited and translated by **William R. Russell.** New York: Penguin Classics, 2017, pp.14-29.

Macleod, Joseph Gordon. *The Ecliptic.* Chicago, IL: Flood Editions, 2016.

Milton, John. *Paradise Lost.* Edited by John Leonard. New York: Penguin Classics, 2003.

Moorcock, Michael. *Elric of Melniboné.* London: Hutchinson, 1972.

Niedecker, Lorine. *Collected Works.* Edited by Jenny **Penberthy.** Berkeley, CA: University of California Press, 2002.

Nitsch, Hermann. "the orgies mysteries theatre." HERMAN NITSCH DAS ORIGIEN MYSTERIEN THEATER, https://www.nitsch.org/en/aktionen/. Accessed 15 June 2023.

O'Leary, Peter and Steven Manuel. "Noticing 6: Interview with Peter O'Leary on THE SAMPO." *Stray Horn: Noticings.* https://stray-horn.blogspot.com/2016/04/noticing-6-interview-with-peter-oleary.html. Accessed 15 June 2023.

Olson, Charles. *The Maximus Poems.* Edited by George F. Butterick. Berkeley, CA: University of California Press, 1983.

Oppen, George. *New Collected Poems.* Edited by Michael Davidson. New York: New Directions, 2002.

Orwell, George. *Animal Farm.* New York: Alfred A. Knopf, 1993.

Palmer, Michael. "Coda: The Open." *Robert Duncan's Legacies: a Centennial Celebration.* https://journals.openedition.org/sillagescritiques/10437. Accessed 15 June 2023.

Palmer, Samuel. *The Letters of Samuel Palmer: Volume 1, 1814-1859.* Edited by Raymond Lister. Oxford: Clarendon Press, 1974.

Pope, Alexander. *The Poems of Alexander Pope. Volume 4: Imitations of Horace, with An Epistle to Dr Arbuthnot, and the Epilogue to the Satires.* Edited by John Butt. London: Methuen & Co. Ltd., 1953.

Pound, Ezra. *The Cantos of Ezra Pound.* New York: New Directions, 1996.

—. ***The Spirit of Romance.*** New York: New Directions, 2005.

Pullman, Philip. *The Secret Commonwealth: The Book of Dust, Volume 2.* New York: Alfred A. Knopf, 2019.

Samperi, Frank. *Trilogy.* Clifton Village, Nottingham: Skysill Press, 2013.

Sewell, Elizabeth. *The Orphic Voice: Poetry and Natural History.* New York: Harper & Row, 1971.

Shelley, Percy Bysshe. *Plato's The Banquet.* Edited by John Lauritsen. Provincetown, MA: Pagan Press, 2001.

—. ***The Complete Poems of Percy Bysshe Shelley.*** New York: The Modern Library, 1994.

"Solar System (Remastered 2000)." *YouTube*, uploaded by The Beach Boys. 21 February 2017. https://youtu.be/LlwOouOHqc0.

Spotlight. Directed by Tom McCarthy. Participant Media / First Look Media / Anonymous Content / Rocklin/Faust Productions / Open Road Films, 2015.

Steiner, Rudolf. *How to Know Higher Worlds.* Hudson, NY: Anthroposophic Press, 1994.

Teskey, Gordon. *The Poetry of John Milton.* Cambridge, MA: Harvard University Press, 2015.

"Thelonious Monk Epistrophy." *YouTube,* uploaded by ajack2boys. 2 July 2013. https://youtu.be/hLopWusx-ZU.

"Thick and Dazzling Darkness." *YouTube*, uploaded by Lumen Christi Institute. 5 March 2018. https://youtu.be/IgVHww_Mh9k.

"What Time Does The Next Miracle Leave?" *YouTube*, uploaded by Frank Sinatra. 28 March 2019. https://youtu.be/ysqW9KKQNh4.

Wittgenstein, Ludwig. *Tractatus Logico-Philosophicus*. Translated by D.F. Pears and B.F. McGuinness. London and New York: Routledge Classics, 2001.

Wordsworth, William. *The Prelude: The Four Texts (1798, 1799, 1805, 1850)*. Edited by Jonathan Wordsworth. New York: Penguin Classics, 1995.

—. **"Yarrow Revisited."** *The Major Works, including The Prelude*. Edited by Stephen Gill. Oxford: Oxford University Press, 1984.

Yates, Frances. *The Occult Philosophy in the Elizabethan Age*. London: Routledge, 2001.

Yeats, W.B. "The Second Coming." *The Collected Poems of W.B. Yeats*. New York: Simon & Schuster, 1996.

"YES – The Gates of Delirium – Live at QPR." *YouTube*, uploaded by yesofficial. 4 October 2014. https://youtu.be/WJRVBQtKltM.

TRILOGY
BIBLIOGRAPHY

NOTE: Books the material from which makes appearances across all three volumes have not been repeated after the first mention.

PHOSPHORESCENCE OF THOUGHT

Aygi, Gennedy. *Field-Russia.* Translated by Peter France. New York: New Directions, 2007.

Bateson, Gregory. *Steps to an Ecology of Mind.* Chicago, IL: University of Chicago Press. 1972.

Benedicite, omnia opera Domini.

Blake, William. *The Complete Poems.* Edited by Alicia Ostriker. New York: Penguin Classics, 1977.

Die große Stille [Into Great Silence]. Directed by Philip Gröning. Zeitgeist Films, 2005.

Dickinson, Emily. *The Poems.* Edited by R.W. Franklin. Cambridge: Harvard University Press, 1999.

Edelman, Gerard M. *Wider than the Sky: The Phenomenal Gift of Consciousness.* New Haven: Yale University Press, 2004.

Emerson, Ralph Waldo. "The Poet." In *Essays & Poems.* New York: Library of America College Editions, 1996.

Euripides. *Bacchae, Iphigenia at Aulis, Rhesus.* Translated by David Kovacs. Loeb Classical Library. Cambridge: Harvard University Press. 2002.

For All Mankind. Directed by Al Reinert. Apollo Associates, 1989.

Goethe, Johann Wolfgang von. *Selected Poetry.* Translated by David Luke. New York: Penguin Classics, 2005.

Graves, Robert. *The Greek Myths: 1 & 2.* New York: Penguin Books, 1960.

James, William. *The Principles of Psychology*, volumes 1 and 2. New York: Dover Publications,1950.

Kerényi, Carl. *Prometheus: Archetypal Image of Human Existence.* Bollingen Series LXV-I. Translated by Ralph Manheim. Princeton: Princeton University Press, 1997.

Kroodsma, Donald. *The Singing Lives of Birds: The Art and Science of Listening to Birdsong.* New York: Harcourt Brace, 2005.

Macdonald, Helen. *Falcon.* London: Reaktion Books, 2006

Matthiessen, Peter. *The Birds of Heaven.* New York: North Point Press, 2001.

Meyer, Thomas. *Staves Calends Legends.* Highlands, North Carolina: Jargon Society, 1979.

The New Testament. Translated by William Tyndale, 1526. London: The British Library, 2000.

Ovid. *Metamorphoses.* Books I-VIII. Translated by Frank Justus Miller; revised by G.P. Goold. Loeb Classics.Cambridge: Harvard University Press, 1984.

—. ***Metamorphoses.*** Books IX-XV. Translated by Frank Justus Miller; revised by G.P. Goold. Loeb Classics. Cambridge: Harvard University Press, 1984.

—. ***Metamorphoses.*** Translated by Mary Innes. New York: Penguin Classics, 1955.

Ovid's Metamorphoses: The Arthur Golding Translation (1567). Edited by John Frederick Nims. New York: Macmillan, 1965.

Rideau, Emile. *The Thought of Teilhard de Chardin.* Translated by René Hague. New York: Harper & Row, 1967.

Schaefer, Vincent J. and John A. Day. *Atmosphere: Clouds, Rain, Snow, Storms.* Peterson Field Guides. Boston: Houghton Mifflin, 1981.

Smart, Christopher. *Selected Poems.* New York: Penguin Classics, 1990.

Swimme, Brian and Thomas Berry. *The Universe Story.* New York: HarperCollins, 1992.

Symeon, the New Theologian, and Johannes Koder. *Hymnes.* Paris: Éditions du Cerf, 1969.

Teilhard de Chardin, Pierre. *The Divine Milieu.* Translated by Bernard Wall. New York: Harper & Row, 1960.

—. *The Making of a Mind: Letters from a Soldier-Priest [1914-1919].* Translated by René Hague. New York: Harper & Row, 1961.

—. *The Phenomenon of Man.* Translated by Bernard Wall. New York: Harper & Row, 1959.

Trakl, Georg. "Helian." In *Das dichterische Werk.* Edited by Walther Killy and Hans Szklenar. Munich: Deutscher Taschenbuch Verlag, 1972.

Whitman, Walt. *Leaves of Grass. Poetry and Prose.* New York: Library of America, 1984.

—. *Selected Poems 1855-1892.* Edited by Gary Schmidgall. New York: St. Martin's Press, 1999.

—. "Words." In *Poems for the Millennium*, volume 3. Edited by Jerome Rothenberg and Jeffrey C. Robinson. Berkeley, CA: University of California Press, 2009.

[**Unknown author and title.** Article on Kirtland's Warblers in *Nature Conservancy*, 56.1 (2006).]

The Odes of Pindar. Translated by Sir John Sandys. Loeb Classical Library. Harvard. Harvard C. Robinson. Berkeley, CA: University of California Press, 2009.

The Odes of Pindar. Translated by C.M. Bowra. New York: Penguin Classics, 1969.

Allegro, John M. *The Sacred Mushroom & the Cross*. New York: Bantam Books, 1971.

Ancient Christian Magic: Coptic Texts of RitualPower. Edited by Marvin Meyer. San Francisco, CA: Harper SanFrancisco, 1994.

Arora, David. *Mushrooms Demystified*. Second Edition. Berkeley, CA: Ten Speed Press, 1986.

"Caedmon's Hymn." *The Wanderers: Elegies, Epics, Riddles.* Translated by Michael Alexander. New York: Penguin Classics, 2008.

Cage, John, with Joan Retallack. *Musicage: John Cage Muses on Words, Art, Music*. Middletown, Connecticut: Wesleyan University Press, 1996.

Dan, Joseph. *Kabbalah: A Very Short Introduction*. Oxford: Oxford University Press, 2004.

Durkheim, Emile. *Elementary Forms of the Religious Life.* Translated by Joseph Ward Swain New York: Free Press, 1965.

Hopkins, Gerard Manley. *Poems*. Edited by Robert Bridges. Oxford: Oxford University Press, 1930.

Hopkins, Gerard Manley, and Humphry House. *The Notebooks and Papers of Gerard Manley Hopkins*. London, New York: Oxford University Press, 1937.

Huffman, D.M., L.H. Tiffany, G. Knaphus, and R.A. Healy, *Mushrooms and Other Fungi of the Midcontinental United States.* Second Edition. Iowa City: University of Iowa Press, 2008.

McFarland, Joe, and Gregory M. Mueller. *Edible Wild Mushrooms of Illinois & Surrounding States.* Urbana: University of Illinois Press, 2009.

Jung, Carl. *The Red Book.* Edited by Sonu Shamdasani. New York: Norton, 2009.

Money, Nicholas P. *Mushroom.* Oxford: Oxford University Press, 2011.

Miller, Orson K., Jr. *Mushrooms of North America.* New York: E.P. Dutton & Co., no date.

The Nag Hammadi Scriptures. Edited by Marvin Meyer. New York: HarperOne, 2007.

Pendell, Dale. *Pharmako Gnosis.* Berkeley, CA: North Atlantic Books, 2010.

Pickard, Tom. *Hole in the Wall.* Chicago, IL: Flood Editions, 2002.

Ramsbottom, John. *Mushrooms & Toadstools.* The New Naturalist. London: Collins, 1953.

Roberts, Peter, and Shelley Evans. *The Book of Fungi.* Chicago, IL: University of Chicago Press, 2011.

Stamets, Paul. *Mycelium Running.* Berkeley, CA: Ten Speed Press, 2005.

Sturluson, Snorri. *Edda.* Translated by Anthony Faulkes. New York: Everyman's Library, 1987.

Thoreau, Henry David. *A Year in Thoreau's Journal: 1851.* New York: Penguin Classics, 1993.

Vaughan, Henry. "The World." *The Meditative Poem.* Edited by Louis L. Martz. Garden City, NY: Anchor Books, 1963.

Wasson, R. Gordon. *Soma: The Divine Mushroom of Immortality.* Ethno-mycological Studies No. 1. New York: Harcourt Brace Jovanovich, no date.

Weil, Andrew M. *The Marriage of the Sun and Moon: Dispatches from the Frontiers of Consciousness.* Boston: Houghton Mifflin, 1998.

The Zohar. Pritzker Edition, volume 1. Translated by Daniel C. Matt. Stanford: Stanford University Press, 2004.

THE HIDDEN EYES OF THINGS

al-Biruni, Abu'l-Rayhan Muhammad Ibn Ahmad. *The Book of Instruction in the Elements of the Art of Astrology.* Astrology Classics 2006.

Allen, Robert Hinckley. *Star Names: Their Lore and Meaning.* New York: Dover, 1963.

Barton, Tamsyn. *Ancient Astrology.* London: Routledge, 1994.

Coppack, Austin, and Daniel A. Schulke. *The Celestial Art: Essays on Astrological Magic.* Three Hands Press, 2018.

Cox, Brian. *Wonders of the Solar System.* London: Collins, 2011.

Cumont, Franz. *Astrology and Religion among the Greeks and Romans.* New York, Dover 1960.

Dionysius (Pseudo-Dionysius). *The Complete Works.* Translated by Colm Luibheid. Classics of Western Spirituality. Mahwah: New Jersey: Paulist Press, 1987.

Ficino, Marsilio. *The Book of Life.* Translated by Charles Boer. Washington, D.C.: Spring Publications 1980.

—. *The Letters of Marsilio Ficino,* volumes I-III. Translated by members of the Language Department of the School of Economic Science, London. London: Gingko Press, 1985.

Gettings, Fred. *The Arkana Dictionary of Astrology.* London: Arkana, 1985.

Gettings, Fred. *The Book of the Zodiac.* London: Triune, 1972.

Hand, Robert. *Horoscope Symbols.* Atglen, Pennsylvania: Whitford Press, 1981.

Hillman, James. *A Terrible Love of War.* New York: Penguin Books, 2004.

Homeric Hymns Homeric Apocrypha Lives of Homer. Translated by Martin L. West. Loeb Classical Library Cambridge: Harvard University Press, 2003.

Innes, Brian. *Horoscopes: How to Draw and Interpret Them.* London: Arco, 1978.

Lucretius. *De Rerum Natura.* Translated by W.H.D. Rouse. Loeb Classical Library. Cambridge: Harvard University Press, 1992.

Manilius. *Astronomica.* Translated by G.P. Goold. Loeb Classical Library. Cambridge: Harvard University Press, 1997.

Plotinus. *The Enneads.* Translated by Stephan MacKenna. New York: Pantheon, 1969.

Rothery, David A. *The Planets: A Very Short Introduction.* Oxford: Oxford University Press, 2010.

Tarnas, Richard. *Cosmos and Psyche: Intimations of a New World View.* New York: Viking 2006.

Wind, Edgar. *Pagan Mysteries in the Renaissance.* London: Faber and Faber, 1958.

...

WORKS BY PETER O'LEARY

BOOKS

Depth Theology. Athens, GA: University of Georgia Press, 2006.

Earth Is Best. Brooklyn: The Cultural Society, 2019.

The Four Horsemen: Poetry and Apocalypse, Brooklyn: The Cultural Society, 2024.

Gnostic Contagion: Robert Duncan and the Poetry of Illness. Middletown, CT: Wesleyan University Press, 2002.

The Hidden Eyes of Things. Brooklyn: The Cultural Society, 2022.

Luminous Epinoia. Brooklyn: The Cultural Society, 2010.

Phosphorescence of Thought. Brooklyn: The Cultural Society, 2013.

The Sampo. Brooklyn: The Cultural Society, 2016.

Thick and Dazzling Darkness: Religious Poetry in a Secular Age. New York: Columbia University Press, 2017.

Watchfulness. Brooklyn: Spuyten Duyvil Press, 2001.

CHAPBOOKS

Benedicite. Chicago, IL: Answer Tag Home Press, 2009.

Icons. Charleston, IL: tel let, 1996.

Midas. New York: Meeting Eyes Bindery / Poetry New York, 1998.

A Mystical Theology of the Limbic Fissure. Loveland, OH: Dos Madres Press, 2005.

Watchfulness. Ellsworth, ME: Backwoods Broadsides Chaplet Series 21, 1996.

Wren / Omen. San Francisco, CA: Albion Books, 2010.

AS EDITOR

Johnson, Ronald. *ARK.* Chicago, IL: Flood Editions, 2013; new edition, 2025.

—. *The Book of the Green Man.* London: Uniformbooks, 2015.

—. *Radi Os.* Chicago: Flood Editions, 2005.

—. *To Do As Adam Did: Selected Poems of Ronald Johnson.* Jersey City, NJ: Talisman House, Publishers, 2000.

—. *The Shrubberies.* Chicago: Flood Editions, 2001.

—. *Valley of the Many-Colored Grasses.* New York: The Song Cave, 2023.

Taggart, John. *Is Music: Selected Poems.* Port Townsend, WA: Copper Canyon Press, 2010.

AUTHOR BIOGRAPHIES

Dan Beachy-Quick is a poet, essayist, and translator. His work has been supported by the Monfort, Lannan, and Guggenheim Foundations. He is Interim Chair of the English Department at Colorado State University where he is a University Distinguished Teaching Scholar.

Billie Chernicoff is the author of five collections of poetry, most recently *Minor Secrets* (Black Square Editions, 2022) and *Amoretti* (Lunar Chandelier Collective, 2020). She lives between the Catskill Creek and the Hudson River.

Norman Finkelstein used to be a professor and almost became a psychoanalyst. His most recent book of poetry is *Further Adventures* (Dos Madres, 2023); his most recent critical work is a volume of selected essays, *To Go Into the Words* (Michigan, 2023). He writes and edits the poetry review blog Restless Messengers.

Elizabeth T. Gray, Jr.'s recent work includes *After the Operation* (Four Way Books 2025), *Salient* (New Directions, 2020), *Let Us Believe in the Beginning of the Cold Season*, translations of Iranian poet Forough Farrokhzad (New Directions, 2022), and *Eighty Ghazals from the Diwán of Háfiz-i Shírází,* (Monkfish Publishing, 2024).

Whit Griffin is a poet-medium currently residing in the Pacific Northwest.

Devin Johnston lives in St. Louis, Missouri. His most recent book of poetry is *Dragons* (Farrar, Straus and Giroux, 2023).

Emily Tristan Jones was raised in the arctic and prairies. Her first book, *Buttercup*, will be published by Verge Books. She lives in Montreal, where she edits *Columba* and teaches poetry to at-risk youth.

Devin King's most recent book is *Gathering* (Kenning Editions, 2023). During the composition of this book he read daily Johnson's *Lives of the Poets* in the Upper Reading Room of the Bodleian Old Library. He now lives in Berkeley, California where he is writing a biography of Ronald Johnson.

Márton Koppány is a Hungarian poet who lost his mother tongue more than forty years ago and is still searching for it.

Steven Manuel has published one book of poetry, *The Fire* (New Books, 2023). He's currently at work on a PhD at Brown University where his dissertation is a critical edition of Ronald Johnson's *ARK: The Foundations*. Presently somewhat alive in Providence, RI.

Thomas Meyer's most recent books are *The Turing Opera* (Hiding Press, 2024) and *Fisher King* (Verge Books 2024). He lives with his Husband Michael Watt on the Solway Firth near the Borderlands of England.

Patrick Morrissey is the author of *The Differences* (Pressed Wafer, 2014), *World Music* (Verge Books, 2017), and *Light Box* (Verge, 2023). He lives in Chicago.

Michael O'Leary is the younger, wiser brother of Peter O'Leary.

Peter O'Leary is the author of *The Hidden Eyes of Things* (The Cultural Society, 2022) and *The Four Horsemen: Poetry and Apocalypse* (The Cultural Society, 2024). He is the editor of Verge Books. He lives in Oak Park, Illinois.

Kylan Rice is the author of *An Image Not a Book* (Parlor Press / Free Verse Editions, 2023) and *Incryptions* (Spuyten Duyvil, 2021) and co-author of *Primer* (Free Poetry, 2023), a collection of conversations with the poet Dan Beachy-Quick. He is co-editor of Thirdhand Books and the associate editor of the *Missouri Review*.

John Tipton lives in Chicago. He is the publisher of Verge Books. His most recent book is *Believers and Seven Sermons from the Bacchae* (Flood Editions, 2022).

Steven Toussaint is the author of the poetry collections *The Bellfounder* (2015) and *Lay Studies* (2019). More recent writing can be found in *Fence, Wild Court, Landfall,* and *Image.* He lives with his family in England.

G.C. Waldrep's most recent books are *feast gently* (Tupelo, 2018), winner of the William Carlos Williams Award from the Poetry Society of America; *The Earliest Witnesses* (Tupelo/Carcanet, 2021); and *The Opening Ritual* (Tupelo, 2024). Waldrep lives in Lewisburg, Pa., where he teaches at Bucknell University.

Stephen Williams is the author of *Earth Enough* (Dos Madres, 2021) and *The Star of the End* (Dos Madres, 2022). He lives in Chicago.

For the full Dos Madres Press catalog:
www.dosmadres.com